TO THE
CORNER

Niall

Heartfelt thanks for the
joy of action week. There
will always be a poem in my
heart for you.

With love and affection
Gen Campbell

TO THE FOUR CORNERS

◆

Exciting and Personal Around-the-World Travel Stories Entwined with Dramatic Historical Episodes

Eugene Weisberger

To Niall,
We missed hearing your
wonderful happy voice at
the book party. Hope you
enjoy my tales
With love
Gene

iUniverse, Inc.
New York Lincoln Shanghai

TO THE FOUR CORNERS
Exciting and Personal Around-the-World Travel Stories Entwined with Dramatic Historical Episodes

Copyright © 2005 by Eugene Weisberger

iUniverse books may be ordered through booksellers or by contacting:

iUniverse
2021 Pine Lake Road, Suite 100
Lincoln, NE 68512
www.iuniverse.com
1-800-Authors (1-800-288-4677)

ISBN-13: 978-0-595-35061-2 (pbk)
ISBN-13: 978-0-595-79767-7 (ebk)
ISBN-10: 0-595-35061-5 (pbk)
ISBN-10: 0-595-79767-9 (ebk)

Printed in the United States of America

Dedication

"To the Four Corners" Is dedicated to my wife of thirty-five years. We have spent those years constructively working together and playing together, sometimes in laughter and sometimes in tears. Each of us had very successful careers, Lila as a school psychologist in a school district in Long Island, New York and, myself, as a business executive for General Instrument Corporation(GI) in the same area. After we retired we both have found new interests to enjoy. For Lila it has been the combining of two loves she has had all her life: poetry and therapy. For me it is an entirely new field: short story writing.

Several years ago she earned her credential as a Poetry Therapist with the National Association of Poetry Therapy.(NAPT). Shortly thereafter, she became president of that organization. Now for the past three years, she is writing essays under a byline entitled "Findings" for the NAPT magazine, Museletter and actively as a mentor supervisor with students working toward their Therapy credentials.

In the fall issue, of 2004, Volume 25, Number 2 she wrote a beautiful story that draws upon our life in a touching and emotional way. I can think of no better way to begin my book than by sharing this story with my readers. Here is Lila's story to a most appreciative husband.

Lila begins this book with the use of a technique more appropriate for the engineer than for the poet. Quickly, however, the poetess in her shines through.

It begins:

"I drew two coordinates on graph paper: height and length, and plotted ten years of my life. My plans altered dramatically upon reading Robert Frost's poem "Happiness Makes Up In Height What It Lacks In Length" and a book by Daniel Stern, "One Day's Perfect Weather: More Twice Told Tales." I yearned to reach a new height on one perfect day yet to come. This experience led to my thrice-told tale.

"My life had been filled with an abundance of perfect days until 1996 when my husband Gene was diagnosed with salivary gland cancer. We hoped this disease would cause us only a slight detour from our long, happy, loving, path. Instead we found ourselves on an unmarked road with only periodic plateaus on which to rest. I graphed out what this looked like, pondering our cyclical, downward spiraling path, so missing of peaks.

"Gene has defied statistics and his doctors call him Lazarus. At a turtle's pace, he has learned to deal with increasing pain as his years and physical limitations multiply. Gene is motivated to travel to exotic places regardless of his pain each year. After 1996 I took only a few trips out of the United States with Gene despite his persistent wish to have me to continue to accompany him on these adventures.

"His medical emergencies were difficult for me to cope with and I did not want to travel with him away from our homeland. This was disappointing to him and he began to travel with friends. One time he had to come back from Prague on an emergency basis and went straight from the airport to Sloan-Kettering Cancer Center where he was hospitalized for five weeks and had three surgeries. Another time in Belize he was bitten by mosquitoes, which were vectors for bot flies, and came back with larva growing under his skin. In Iceland, his travel companion had to get him to the Emergency Room in the middle of the night and then find a way for them to catch up with their tour group. Gene's many close calls reinforced my decision not to travel with him out of the U.S. He considered these events as stories he could write about; I considered them nightmares.

"Gene has become a writer and uses the material he gathers from his travels as material for his stories. His first book is "The Chinese Walking Stick and Other Stories," and his second is "Lazarus from 7 to 77." Gene is currently working on his third book of short stories. The excitement he feels when researching and planning complex itineraries, and then the adventure of meeting new people, and seeing places he has only read about thrills him, like how he loved seeing the pyramids in Egypt, although much of the trip, he was in a wheelchair. Still he descended into the pyramid energized by his will power. After each trip he spends days in bed writing his stories on his lap top computer.

"Gene is determined to travel to a small hamlet in Germany in the Black Forest to visit and tour with Anemone, a friend he made in a writing group arranged by www.Litkicks.com. Gene and Anemone have formed a tight friendship and he writes to her nightly and she to him often the next day. Unfortunately, none of his travel buddies are available to take this trip with him. Anemone invited us to stay at her home in Germany and Gene accepted this invitation even if he would travel by himself, which is not advisable. I could not bring myself to consider taking this trip with him.

"Now the Frost poem—O stormy, stormy world/were days so very few/one days perfect weather/the day swept clearly on/to finish clear at eve.

In Daniel Stern's story a couple are reading the very poem by Frost that these lines are quoted from. This story is about a young couple who know that their life together will soon end because the man has only a short time left to live. The couple discuss Frost's poem and decide to get out of bed and to give themselves and each other the gift of one perfect day.

"I cried when reading this story and poem, and I questioned myself to see if I had the courage and fortitude to give Gene 'one perfect day.' I hoped that the gift giving in itself would give me a gift: the ability to stretch to meet this challenge. I am aware of the pressure his illness puts on me, and my need to protect myself and look away. Nevertheless, I was joyful at the possibility of giving him the best gift I could while he could accept it. This gift giving would be a height for me and traveling together again would be a height for both of us. I could not dilly dally waiting for a more perfect time. I want to 'carpe diem' and thus will stretch to a fuller height.

"So in mid September we shall have our perfect day. (Will we???) His/our joy started when I told him of my gift to him. I told him that I would go to

Germany with him to tour and visit with Anemone I am thankful that the poem by Robert Frost and story by Gerald Stern brought the concepts of height and length to my consciousness. These works raised me to a new height. I faced the fact that I don't have length to wait so as to find a more perfect time on our 'graph'."

And so this book is dedicated to a wonderful and selfless wife whom I love more every day. The art she has mastered like no one else I have ever known, is one of listening. This has made her a wonderful teacher and a loving friend to me and all who know her. Through her understanding of others, I have found out what being a excellent poet really is. You do not have to make two words rhyme to have such a talent. It is the feeling that comes from down deep in your soul that makes someone a great poet. Lila is a great poet; a poet of the soul. Lastly, she understands the meaning of sacrifice and practices it as an art. I learn more from her then I possibly could have imagined and my continued goal is to be worthy of having Lila as my wife.

Contents

PREFACE. xv

PROLOGUE 1

INTRODUCTION 5

CHAPTER I   Alexander's World—The Beginning of
                Civilization 11

- *ISRAEL*. *12*
  1. The Promised Land: 12
  2. The Scene Changes 16
  3. The Tale Of The Tzitzis 17
- *GREECE* *19*
  4. Costa's Magical Spirit 19
  5. The Problem with Sailing the Aegean. 21
- *YUGOSLAVIA/ALBANIA:* *22*
  6. The Death of Communism Along the Adriatic. 22
- *TURKEY* *24*
  7. Ancient Ephesus: Where East Meets West 24
  8. Dinner in Ankara. 27
  9. Turkey: Downhill 28
- *EGYPT*. *30*
  10. The Gift of the Nile 30
- *BULGARIA* *34*
  11. A Funny Thing Happened On The Way To Bulgaria. 34
- *UKRAINE* *36*
  12. A Gift For Odessa 36

13. Yalta: Remembering FDR 38

• *RUSSIA* *40*

14. Russian Rules and Regulations 40

• *POLAND* *42*

15. Forever Amber 42

CHAPTER 2   Caesar's Conquests 44

• *France* *44*

1. The Mediterrean Surprise 44

2. First Address in Western Europe 47

3. The ABC's of Southern France 50

4. Les Beau Dynasty 56

5. The Cathedral Of Images 59

6. Department 46—A Secret Hideaway 61

7. The Caves of Pech Merle 64

8. The Room At Monet's Place 67

9. Paris: The City of Beauty 69

10. The Oktoberfest 72

11. Time Out for Germany 73

12. A Breath of Fresh Air "On The Road To The Black Forest" 75

13. Munstertal, A String of A Town 77

14. Experiencing the Black Forest 78

15. More Than Just a Book Fair 81

• *Iceland* *83*

16: Worth a Trip From Anywhere 83

17. A Prayer For Bergen 86

• *Ireland* *89*

18. A Relaxed and Friendly Country 89

• *United Kingdom* *94*

19. "Yes, Gene, where are our seats?" 94

20. The Falkland's Coincidence 96

CHAPTER 3   Marco's Travels 99

1. Training In China 99

2. The Yangtze River Sunrise 102

3. A Pair of Swinging Bridges 105

4. Terra Cotta Figures Come to Life 107

6. Leshan's Giant Buddha 111

6. Sociology: 102 113

•   *Taiwan* *115*

7. Taiwan To Suit 115

9. The GI Party At The Grand 118

10. Dinner For Two In Osaka 121

CHAPTER 4   COLUMBUS' DISCOVERIES 123

1. The Caribbean: Then and Now— 123

•   *UNITED STATES/CANADA* *125*

2. Key West: A Favorite Picture 125

3. Murder at Marathon Key 130

4. The Quiet, Running Everglades 132

5. Savannah and Her Squares 134

6. Historic Charleston 135

7. Three Bonsai Gardens 137

8. Quebec—The Old Town 140

9. Traveling in Groups 142

10. The Many Views of The Golden State 143

11. California's Garden of Eden 145

12. Yosemite—Half Dome from Many Angles 147

13. Yosemite—El Capitan's Diamonds 150

14. Washington: Remembered & Rediscovered 151

EPILOGUE 155

ACKNOWLEDGMENTS

With deep appreciation, I acknowledge the great effort of Marie Fenton Griffing and Johanna Martinez who worked so diligently with me to assemble and edit this manuscript. Without their effort, this book would never have come to fruition. I would like to acknowledge the wonderful front cover design of my daughter-in-law, Jacki Weisberger. Her design showed great imagination and ingenuity. It most assuredly added to the demeanor of the book. I would also like to acknowledge all the tour guides who introduced me to the wonders of the world.

To help guide you through this book, I have compiled the names of my friends and associates as they appear in my stories. I sincerely thank them for joining me in my travels, sometimes sharing my aches and pains, and for allowing me to use their names in this book.

LET ME INTRODUCE YOU TO:

Lila—my loving wife and travel companion
All the children, and grandchildren mentioned at various times
throughout the book . They know how much I care.
Dr. Hohl_ Sloan Kettering M. D. who treated my infection
Costa—Greek business representative, Athens
Jim Adams & Dotty—Vice President of Marketing, General Instrument (and successor to me as General Manager, Government Systems Division) and wife
Joe Burros—my cousin, traveling companion and dear friend
Abdullah—Egyptian guide from Cairo
Leila—Pyramid tour guide
Elias & Genny—Greek Air Force consultant and wife from Athens
Carl—Ukranian emigrant
Robert, Carol & Katie—Joe's friends from California & Southern France
Anemone, Bernd & Zora—dear friends from Munstertal, Germany
Ari—tour guide in Iceland
Marty Goodstone—friend and travel partner, Long Island, N. Y.
Don White—Vice President, Undersea Systems Div., General Instrument

Key Young Chung—South Korean business representative
Judy & Phil—tour guide and husband in the Falkland Islands
May Wah & Julie Zhu—tour guides on our first trip to China
    Julie became our god-daughter and her family are like ours
Phyllis & Tom—old friends from Long Island, NY who traveled with us in China
Baochen Zhu (Julie's father) & Heather—travel guides on our second trip to China
Moses Shapiro (Monty)—CEO of General Instrument
Jim Klein & Helen—President, General Instrument, Taiwan and wife
Frank Hickey & George Safiol—General Instrument Executives
Tom Takano—Japanese business representative, from Tokyo
The McGraths—couple encountered on Carribean cruise
Bena—Joe's friend with whom we traveled in Key West
Leo-Taxi drive/guide in Quebec
Leon Singer—Florida acquaintance who I encountered in Palm Springs, CA
Robert Settle—pool service man who shared a travel story

PREFACE

Meanings Of The Four Corners

There are many meanings of 'the four corners' and in the process of writing this book, I came upon some of them. Long before the four corners referred to directions, they had other meanings. Used by ancient peoples mostly throughout the British Isles, they referred to the elemental needs that were necessary for survival. In the early days of civilization, people like the Druids referred earth, air, fire and water as the four corners; the necessities for their continued existence. In addition to 'corners', they were also called 'quarters', watchtowers', 'elements' or 'elementals'. Since they did not know where these materials came from, there was much mysticism and witchcraft practiced in their use.

Then with the advent of the magnetic compass and the development of the four cardinal points of direction, the original elements became associated with the new directional points. North became associated with earth or land—East with fire or air; South also with air or fire, and lastly, West with water. The pagan people of Ireland and Britain often held ceremonies or rituals to pray over the elements to insure their continue existence. This was especially true with fire and water.

Coming over to the Western Hemisphere and its development, there is an area where the states of Colorado, Utah, Arizona and New Mexico meet, which has become known as the four corners. Historically it is the location where the Anasazi Indians lived hundreds of years ago. In that approximate area there once were many multi-story stone dwellings (pueblos) where these people lived from about 300 A.D. to 1300 A.D. Then mysteriously they disappeared with little or no trace of why and under what circumstances they left. Recently archeologists have been studying the reason, and now it is a tourist attraction. I never had the opportunity to see that 'four corners site'. Nevertheless, this is another meaning of the phrase.

In the case of national sports there is another meaning for the four corners. In the Southeastern Basketball Conference there was one team that consistently did better than the rest. For over a decade North Carolina State, coached by Dean Smith, dominated their conference. The team was always so much better than the competition that they would jump off to an early lead in almost every game. As soon as they were sufficiently ahead, they would use a technique of putting one man in each corner of the court and pass the ball back without shooting for the hoop. The other team, frustratingly, could not even get a chance to score. The technique was soon given the name "the four corners." Incidentally, it was for this reason that the basketball rules were changed to require each team to shoot for the hoop within a given number of seconds after taking possession of the ball.

One day I was talking to several doctors at Sloan Kettering Hospital about my new book. When I told them the name and the fact that so many meanings exist for the phrase—the four corners, Doctor Hohl said that he had yet another meaning. He said the four corners in the medical profession, meant the four hospitals surrounding York Avenue and 68th Street in Manhattan's East Side. "How was this?" I asked. He said that it meant the four Hospitals centered at or near that corner, namely: Sloan Kettering, Rockefeller Institute, Hospital for Special Surgery and New York Cornell Medical Center. He said these four hospitals had the reputation of being the finest in the world. I whole-heartedly agree.

You will read about another of my encounters with the four corners in Chapter One of this book. Because, in the Jewish religion, our people were chased from Jerusalem by the Romans over two thousand years ago, it has been said that they were scattered to the four corners (in Hebrew, arba Kamphot) of the world. Even though they were dispersed and consequently weakened as a race and nationality, I believe it was their determination coupled with certain rituals and symbols that have helped them to survive.

One custom that has stayed with the Jewish people is the wearing of the tallis. The Jews by wearing the tallis (with the tzitzis) helped to remind them that in spite of the fact that they were dispersed to the four corners, they would continue to exist as a people. A tallis is typically a blue and white silk prayer shawl worn by Jewish men over the age of thirteen, who have been bar mitzvahed. . The shawl has a fringe of many silk threads on either end. These tassels have a very particular characteristic.

On either end are two special tassels, for a total of four, that have been given a unique name, tzitzis (see Chapter One, Number 3). history and and the meanings of this phrase, so I have woven it into my own personal tales.

As I traveled thoughout the world, it intrigued me that there are so many interesting tales connected with the history and the different meanings of 'four corners', so appropriately, I have coined those words for the title of my book.

PROLOGUE

Four Threads That Bind our Universe

Over the three thousand years of modern civilization most of mankind has been rather stationary. Typically people have been born, raised and died without traveling more than fifty miles from their birthplace. Traveling has been a rather scary proposition for humans. Dangers confronted men at every turn. Starvation, thirst, tides and disease were just few of man's discouragements. But, in my way of thinking, there have been four great travelers who despite these obstacles, covered as much of their world as was known to them at the time: Alexander the Great, Julius Caesar, Marco Polo, and Christopher Columbus. The history books credit Alexander the Great of Macedonia as the first traveler of civilization. He traveled east to India and then south to Egypt before dying at the very early age of thirty-one from venereal disease.

Alexander's armies had to battle enemies who were determined to stop his aggressive path toward the wealth of India. His path sewed the thread that connected Europe and Asia over twenty-five centuries ago. From his exploits followed the traders who carried the goods between these two continents. This was the beginning of the powerful society that was to become the Greek Empire.

But slowly they lost their world domination to the land across the Adriatic Sea. Five hundred years later, at about 40 B. C. came Julius Caesar and the Roman Empire. He and his armies traveled west and north to as far as the British Isles and developed a new world of power and influence. To this day there are signs of his empire including the cities his legions developed all over Europe. But as with Alexander, Caesar also met an untimely death. Jealousy ambition and power influenced his friend, Brutus, to take Caesar's life. But this leader of his time had sewed the threads of civilization so that traders now went west from Rome and Greece to exchange their goods.. The Roman legions had opened the path to Western Europe sewing another piece of the tapestry of civilization. They built hundreds of towns, villages and cities throughout what is now France, Germany, Great Britain and Spain. All over these countries I have come upon Roman baths, castles, aqueducts and even sewage systems that bear the imprint of Julius Caesar and his men. From the town of Bath in western England to the ancient castle of Staufen, Germany there are signs of the once powerful Roman Empire.

After the fall of the Roman Empire the western world was made up of dozens of little fiefdoms ruled by princes but influenced by the Roman catholic church. Trade between peoples was mainly in western Europe but gradually brave young people began to look to the east, to the orient for new trading possibilities.

Then, during the thirteenth century, a young Venecian, Marco Polo, with his courageous family traveled across the huge continent of Asia to reach the land of China. They came back with wondrous tales, which started once again advancing the threads of civilization. It is said this little man gave China its name. When Marco returned to Venice, he was asked what to call the country. He said, that some travelers call it Cathey, but since its first ruler, who unified the country about one thousand years before, was named Emperor Qin. it could be called Chin's land. Now, in Italian, since everything ends with a vowel, it became China. He spent years in China eventually becoming the minister to Kubla Khan and brought back the knowledge of fireworks, printing presses and dozens of other innovations, including spaghetti.

At the end of the fifteenth century, or three hundred years after Marco Polo, it took another Italian, Christopher Columbus, to reach the remaining one half of our planet, tying this thread of civilization. We all know the story of Columbus and his crew sailing in three little wooden ships braving the winds and tides of the Atlantic until he reached a land he knew nothing about. Actually the Western Hemisphere was already occupied with hundreds of thousands of people: Native Americans, we now call them, who were productively living on this great land. They did not seem to have any desire to go off its shores, and were quite content living on the lands where they grew all the food they needed for their sustenance. The basic difference between the Native Americans and the emigrating people was one of ambition. In the fifteenth and sixteen centuries the Europeans were interesting in exploring the world. The Native Americans were satisfied with their existence. So it was that the men like Columbus sailed the oceans to find out more about their planet and entered upon the world of the Native American.

To me, Columbus, last of the four great travelers was representative of those many adventurers who bound our planet by means of the threads of travel. It is interesting to note, all of them came from around the Mediterranean Sea and three of them actually were born on the Italian peninsular; Julius in Rome, Marco in Venice and Christopher in Genoa.

As I think back on my traveling experiences, the first trip that Lila and I took to the old world was Italy. I was not angry at the Romans for chasing my forefathers out of Jerusalem. In those days, during the 1970's, before I was sophisticated about traveling, we signed up for a tour with that famous tour operator, Perillo. He was not a discoverer of new worlds but rather an entrepreneur. Perillo decided to establish a travel company after the end of WW2. He began by taking people to the country he knew best—Italy, which certainly makes sense from a business point-of-view. The other good business idea he had was to give the average middle-income couple an economical opportunity to visit Europe. Many of his first clients were ex-military people who had been to Europe during the war and wanted to go back to show their families where they had served. He gave the first-time travelers a lot for their money. The three-city tour we took, to Rome, Florence and Venice was indeed the best for the least. We stayed in economy hotels and often traveled in buses that were not air-conditioned.

The part of the trip, that was very special however, were the sights and sounds. What we saw are some of the threads of history that made this land so important to modern civilization. In Rome we walked around the two thousand-year-old Coliseum where gladiators fought and died for the entertainment of the emperors. We stood with reverence in the Vatican's St. Peters Basilica, and what a thrill it was, to hear Pope John Paul bless an audience of over five thousand including, no doubt, other Jews like ourselves. We then walked to the other side of the Vatican to see the Sistene Chapel ceiling, where Michelangelo had painted man reaching out to the hand of God. We climbed the Spanish steps in the heart of Rome, where Julius Caesar lived and died.

Then in Florence we walked around that city with its red roofs and statues of grandeur. My favorite were three statues done by Michelangelo that tied the old to the new testaments. We walked up to the foot of the statue of David, who Jews consider one of our first real leaders from the time that shepherd boy slew the giant, Goliath. This statue stands majestically in front of the Florence museum and depicts David holding the most famous of ancient weapons, the slingshot. From the statue of David, one could say with tongue in cheek, it is just a stone's throw to where Moses resides with his most famous of original laws, the Ten Commandments. Then one goes just a few feet further to Christianity's most impressive statue, the Pieta, the infant Christ held by his mother, Mary. Michelangelo sure was one busy fellow.

From Florence we took the bus to the third of the most important Italian cities, Venice. Rome has its history, Florence its art, but Venice has its romance. There is nothing like walking across one of its four hundred bridges hand in hand with the one you love. The romance of Venice continued as we heard the singing gondoliers on the way to the Grand Canal. It was just breathtaking.

Lila and I sat among fifty other travelers on our Perillo tour as the ten gondolars slowly moved down the Grand Canal. At the rear of each boat stood a gon-
dolier who sang in unison with the others the famous song 'O Solo Mio'. With
each stroke their voices rang to sky on that heavenly evening I shall never forget. I
wondered if Marco Polo ever told the Chinese about his beautiful city if, in the
thirteenth century the Grand Canal had gondolars plying Venice's watery pas-
sages and that romantic couples would enjoy such moments.

Then I thought, how fortunate I will be, if I could see more of the world that
Alexander, Julius, Marco and Columbus never saw. But there, in the year, 1979,
we were coming from Columbus's birthplace, having seen Julius's historic city
and Marco's romantic city and what a wonderful trip it had been. One year later,
I would be seeing Alexander's center of his universe, Athens. It is as if I were traveling along a silken thread woven by the four brave men of civilization. Now, for
more than a quarter of a century, I have traveled to over fifty other countries and
six continents. I have met my own expectations, to be sure, and followed the
threads that tie our civilization into a beautiful magic carpet.

INTRODUCTION

One day as I visited the travel section of a bookstore. I realized how many travel books lined its shelves. I decided that I wanted to write the different travel book, the book that will differentiate my travel stories from the others. It would be similar to my first travel book," The Chinese Walking Stick", yet different because of my using four historical travelers as a theme. The stories will have interpersonal feelings about the places I visited interspersed with various interesting aspects of history, psychology, and sociology. There will be so much more than Frommer's guide books on restaurants, hotels and art galleries. Some travel books do have the history of a country but they do not have the personal aspect. As you read my book you will recognize the interesting difference.

In the beginning you will find some of the tales that I experienced during my working career. From the first trip to Israel, then to Greece and Turkey I found the Middle Easterners so very interesting and exciting. Their sallow complexions and dark black hair gave them a very different look from most of the central and northern Europeans. They also acted quite differently. They more outspoken and I believe less sophisticated.

In the second chapter (Caesar's Conquests) you will find many interesting tales that still refer to Caesar and the Roman leaders from the days of their conquests. I found it interesting there are so many references to the Roman Empire in this part of Europe. But long before the Roman Empire, Southern Europe began the development of its civilization along the coast of the Mediterranean. It all began in and around the caves of Pech Merle with the Cro-Magnon people. It intrigued me that art could have begun on the walls twenty thousand years ago.

Joe and I spent an exciting day traveling down along the very chilly paths where prehistoric Cro-Magnon people told their tale through the writings on the walls. I was most impressed with the wall painting of the ancient horse because it was so much like the horse of today. Around the mural of the horse there were six handprints of what must have been the earliest artist signature known. The handprints are in poor condition near the bottom of the mural but seem to be in much better condition at eye level.

Our guide told us that modern archeologists believe that the prehistoric man would take charcoal from their fires moistened with water and then put the mixture in their mouths. They would place their hand, outstretched to the wall and blow the mixture from their mouth to the surface. The resultant charcoal imprint would then show the image of their hand. We were shocked to hear that those hand impressions could be over eighteen thousand years old. In addition to the horse there were at least six other wall murals carbon-dated to within 18,000 to 20,000 years old. Then there were some footprints that were baked into the muddy ground which also were from that time period. I wondered if any of Julius Caesar's men ever found their way to those caves.

One of the places that I was very impressed with in Western Europe was the ancient city of Glanum. We saw how the buildings in those days actually had their owner's names inscribed in the front stone. One such home had the corner stone engraved with the name (Augustus Caesar). Joe and I walked the narrow streets of Glanum with its marble and stone houses, temples, statues, and immortalized tombs. One aspect that was so interesting was the gutters on each side of the paved streets. They were built on a slope so that when it rained the water would wash down the underground roadway and by the natural force of gravity would clean the system—ingenious, these Romans.

They were careful to keep the clean water system separate from the sewage system. It was amazing to us how they knew the importance of the separation of water and sewage for health reasons. Also they kept the burial grounds outside the city for both religious and sanitary reasons.

But, even with these very important and modern concepts, as if by magic, (black, that is), the entire area of Glanum disappeared beneath the world of the dark ages.

There are interesting stories about Central Europe/Western Asia, one of the most important growth centers of our culture. The country now called Turkey is the gateway between Asia and Europe but was the path of dozens of civilizations in the past three thousand years.

One fine day I took a trip into a museum in Ankara, Turkey that told the story of almost six thousand years of people moving back and forth on the road to modern times. There were the Babylonians, the Persians, the Greeks, the Ottomans, and now modern Turkey that just became a republic in 1923. Later you will read the interesting story of my representative and his life in Ankara.

In Chapter Three you will find me on Marco Polo's trail. He must have found China just as intriguing as I did. China and the Chinese people are some of the most colorful, interesting people on earth. When Marco Polo arrived in the thirteenth century, he found the Chinese were farther advanced in many aspects than the Europeans. They were much ahead in the areas of education and the development of civil service.

They were also advanced in certain areas of technology, like explosives and printing presses. Another element of their society I found most interesting was their social skills. The family unit was, and still is, a very important element in the Chinese culture. For the last two millenniums, members of many families have been living together with a greater level of harmony than in most other civilized centers of the world. They would never consider sending their senior members off to nursing homes. All ages live together—often in small quarters—for their entire lives. The usual routine is for the senior generation to take care of the little kids while the middle generations are the bread winners.

As Marco Polo was so impressed with these people and their land, so it was that I was totally intrigued with the culture and its beauty. A most incredible aspect of this country is its predominant usage of huge numbers of people. Every place we traveled there were ten people doing work that would take only two to do in Europe and the United States.

China always had huge surpluses of children that resulted in more families who had to be put to work in every quarter of society. Since there was no unemployment or old age insurance, the people often were given "make work" projects to keep them busy, otherwise the society would go broke. Everywhere I went I saw these armies of workers. No effort was made until the last two generations to improve employee efficiency.

Now, of course, we know they are trying to reduce the rate of childbirth. Also they are beginning to improve the work efficiency. During our many trips to China and Taiwan, where the people have very similar work ethics but somewhat more advance, I found both countries so excitingly different from ours.

Traveling around a country gives the tourist a better view of the country than staying in just one location. We found that cruising down the Yangtzi River gave the tourist a wonderful view of the magnificent sights like the Three Gorges, the Danning River Rapids or the Wuhan irrigation. In addition we were able to see scores of little villages along the Yangtzi River front. In a few days, we were able to get a vivid picture of what it is to live in a small river front town. One day we sailed along the Li River and had the wonderful experience of seeing the limestone cliffs in and around Guilan.

Another means of transportation was traveling by train around the country. But of course there was nothing like traveling in a car or bus on the dirty, jammed crowded roads. There were thousands of bicycles, motorbikes, three-wheel carts, buses, cars and taxis all jumbled together like nothing you have ever seen. Although Marco never saw motorized vehicles, there must have been all kinds of rickshaws, horses and other beasts of burden in the thirteenth century similar to the crowded roads of the twentieth. My stories will intrigue, excite and urge you to make the trip to the Orient.

Chapter Four covers the part of the world which has changed over the centuries more than any other on our planet—North America. Before Columbus even conceived of traveling to the "New World", North America was inhabited by tens of thousands of native tribes. They survived on the bounty of the earth; they moved from place to place with the seasons and changing weather patterns.

Then came Christopher Columbus and other Spanish explorers to explore this vast continent. They were followed by the Dutch, French and British and eventually changed the entire way of life in this land. Instead of being nomadic people, the Europeans brought in the concept of permanent cities. Within a short period of about two hundred years, the continent had the most drastic change of face in the history of the world.

The Europeans came by the tens of thousands while the diseases they brought in destroyed the natives by the thousands. The people changed so many things but I am happy they left much of the natural beauty, and that I found the strength and time to see many of these places. The stories in Chapter four will take you to some of them. The natural beauty represented by places such as the Everglades, Yellowstone National Park and Yosemite has fortunately remained quite the same because of the foresight of men like John Muir, Theodore Roosevelt and Lewis and Clark.

Traveling throughout the country, I visited those places that were carved out by men like Oglethorpe in Georgia, Williams in Rhode Island, John Adams in Massachusetts. The tales will take you throughout much of North America.

In this lengthy introduction, I hope you have obtained a sense of what is to come in the following pages—and I hope you enjoy your travels to the four corners with me.

Lila and Gene at the Great Wall

1

Alexander's World—The Beginning of Civilization

One thousand years before one of my favorites, Alexander The Great, moved through Asia Minor and into India, a major thriving community lived on a idyllic island now called Crete. Our cruise ship, the Stella Solarus, left Piraeus on the coast of Greece for a ten-day trip around the Aegean Sea. One of the highlights of the trip was a land tour to the ancient palace of the Mineon people, called Knossos, on the island of Crete. My wife, Lila, and I landed in the center of the island and took an hour ride across the farmland of the island until we reached the archeological site. There were a dozen tour buses there before us so I knew it must be an important place to visit.

We entered the site to see many walls with murals that had been dug up in the past one hundred years. It was very clear that this was an important finding. The Minoans who lived on this island were already deep into agriculture that had begun to flourish over three thousand years before. Around the Knossos Palace were many small farms that had thriving communities with groves of olives and grapes. One of the first series of rooms that had been dug up had hundreds of earthenware jars, which must have stored wine and grapes for ceremonial holidays. The gods of the times and the kings were almost intertwined as can be seen by the murals found on the walls. We walked around the huge palace area where dozens of rooms had been excavated. Our guide told us that even in those ancient times the Minions had developed an advanced separate water system that carried fresh water for drinking and below it, a sewerage system that carried away the waste.

Clearly, this was a very developed society for hundreds of years. But then somehow the Minion culture disappeared about five hundred years before the birth of Christ, somewhat like the Mayan people disappeared in Central America around 700 A. D.

One theory was that cities around the palace did not have protection from their enemies who might have come from mainland Europe such as Greece in the north, or Egypt from the south. The Minoans, sitting on this very central island between Europe and Egypt, were extremely successful traders, traveling between these two cultures for hundreds of years. Then it is assumed one of them, probably the Greeks, captured this kingdom and imprisoned the royalty, enslaved the populous and gradually destroyed the palace. Historians believe that the Minion royalty felt very secure in their geographical position, surrounded by the sea, and therefore did not need an army. It always amazed me how many cultures disappeared during those ancient days. Most of them did not have a written language so their histories, cultures, and religious rituals have to a great extent just disappeared.

It is now being left to the archeologists to put together the mysteries of those ancient times. I find it great fun to visit places like Knossos and listen to guides tell us about what the "detectives of the past" have found for us to think about. Having traveled in Egypt and Greece and then seeing the island of Crete I learned how the peoples of those two cultures sailed around the Mediterranean and often stopped off in Crete to trade goods. The archeologists have found hundreds of similar jars in Athens and Karnak like the ones that stored wine in Crete. These "students of the past" have found the same items in other locations around the Aegean Sea proving that trading existed in the Mediterranean area over three thousand years ago.

Visiting Knossos was an exciting trip indeed and on the way back to our ship we stopped off at the museum in Iraklion to see hundreds of items that have been excavated from the royal site and now stored for posterity in the vaults of the museum on this exciting island of Crete.

ISRAEL

1. The Promised Land:

I landed at Ben Gurion Airport outside of Tel Aviv on a bright beautiful autumn day. The plane taxied to the far end of the tarmac and its four huge engines ground to a silent stop. The plane was at least a quarter-mile from any building. Everyone just sat waiting for the usual search and inspection. It was in the late seventies and Israel was on the usual alert for bombs and terrorists, long before terrorism became "fashionable" in our country.

I had been in Athens for almost a month now as we worked on the installation of the first Hellenic Air Force contract. Lila had been in Athens with me for less than a week when she decided that she had enough of Greece and wanted to pay a visit to Israel.

This was my first trip to the country that had become the salvation of the Jews from all over the world. Israel was to be the safe haven for Yemenite Jews, Iranian Jews, Russian Jews, Moroccan Jews and so many oppressed people from the four corners of the world. After the Holocaust and the incredible murder of over six million of Jewish people, Israel was to be the haven to which Jews from all over the world could come, so that such an act of ultimate terrorism would never happen again.

It was incredible to think that now I was here in Israel. Not to reside myself but to visit the land of my forefathers—the land that I studied about when I went to Hebrew school—the land which is the center of so much strife for the last half century, and in the middle of it all I was going to visit Jerusalem.

Israel to me was two very different countries within its little borders. There was the modern day hustle and bustle of modern Tel Aviv and outside the walls of Jerusalem—the modern apartments that cost one million or more. Then there was the old historic City of Jerusalem that centers around the walls of that ancient city and along the Dead Sea to Masada.

At last our plane received its clearance and I stepped off for the very first time on the land where my forefathers had been chased twenty centuries ago. I walked out into the warm air and found a cab that would take me to Tel Aviv and where I had planned to meet Lila. She was staying at a small hotel, near the Mediterranean Sea, and we would stay there for the few days before moving on to Jerusalem. We had not seen each other for a fortnight since she left me working in Athens.

But now the work was behind me and I planned to enjoy every moment in this historic land. From the very first night, as we walked along the Mediterranean that October evening, I felt as though I was home.

When I had visited Athens and saw the Acropolis, the agora and all those ancient ruins, I was reliving history but when I was in Israel, I felt like I was home.

By the time I visited the land of my forefathers I had already been to a dozen countries in central Europe, but visiting Israel was so different.

Everyone you walked past was Jewish. Everybody in the restaurant where we ate dinner was Jewish. I was in the land of Jews, my people. I had never thought of what it would feel like to be in the land of Jews. The best way I know of expressing the feeling was that I felt comfortable.

I knew I would never actually move there. I was too used to the standard of living in the U. S. A. I had too many family ties to leave and resettle in Israel. But being in Israel was a good feeling. A feeling that I had in no other country I had ever visited before or since. Israel was some place special.

When we reached Jerusalem four days later the feeling became even more intense. Not only was it the land of Jewish people from today, but also from the ancient days gone by. I could not get over the fact that I was standing on the ground that King Solomon and King David walked on. Is it possible that twenty-five hundred years ago this was the land of my forefathers? This was the earth that my ancestors trod upon. Could I be touching a stone from the ancient temple of my forefathers? Was I breathing in the air that was inhaled by those people that would have been my family?

Then I thought—where did my ancient family members go after they were chased from this city? How did they get from Israel to Austria and Germany. It would be interesting and exciting to know of their route. Would they have been chased from Jerusalem to North Africa and then, to Spain, then one thousand years ago leave Spain and resettle in Germany? Or were they chased up north into Lebanon, and maybe into Turkey, then into Greece and further into Romania and finally into Austria-Hungary. As I walked along the old wall of Jerusalem I thought of all the generations of people who would eventually become Weisberg-ers of today.

What were the names of those ancient relatives of mine? Were they at one time, in Greece, or maybe Spain, which route did they take before they finally arrived at the shores of the United States? Is it possible that any of my trips in the last three decades cross any of my ancestors' travels? Now as I write of my trips around the four corners of the world I think of all the places my ancestors may also have traveled before reaching the promised land in the twentieth-century.

But then as I walked across the large courtyard in Jerusalem from the Western Wall, I reached the new buildings of the old city. It was such a contrast to see those beautiful modern homes that many orthodox Jews are now living in, and the Arab sections with their very narrow streets and their smelly stalls selling the racks of lamb in shacks two thousand years old. We then walked one of the most famous of all streets where Jesus was to have taken his last walk carrying his cruci-fix. Our last stop was said to be the burial place of King David. The three days in Jerusalem were some of the most impressive in all of my travels.

Then next day we went to Masada, the ancient historical site where over nine hundred Jews were said to have taken their lives rather than surrendering to the Roman legions. I think that this visit was again most impressive.

We drove along the Dead Sea and stopped off to float upon this most unusual of all bodies of water. The water is so full of chemicals, especially sodium, one just floats on it as if one were floating on air. It is an exciting experience—as long as you do not rub your eyes. The salt makes them very irritated I found out, the hard way.

After our one-hour swim we continued on to the base of the cable car that takes you to the top of the mountain. We decided to take the cable car up and then hike down. The cab takes you to within ten feet of the top and you walk those last few feet. The level just beneath the top of Masada is called the reservoir. It is where the water was stored for drinking and washing in order for them to survive.

We spent an hour or so walking along the top studying where those brave people lived and died. From the top we could look down and see where the Romans had their encampment, where they built the ramp to get up to the top and finally make it over the walls. Imagine their surprise and astonishment to find that every single one of those brave souls took their lives rather than to be taken prisoner.

One of the local tour guides then told us that the modern day soldiers now get their commissions while standing on the top of Masada. It must be quite an impressive ceremony to receive your officer's commission while standing on top of Masada. One does not have to be given any words, only think of those brave people who gave their lives rather then to give in to oppression and tyranny. The act says it all.

And so, two thousand years ago the Roman legions marched back to Jerusalem and tried to put a victorious spin on what was a moral defeat. The little force of Jews had beat them psychologically if not militarily. Now what was the power country of Rome to do with people of Jerusalem who believed in this one almighty God who seemed to be everywhere? Hadrian came up with a solution. "Let us divide them chase them out of Jerusalem because so long as they are together they gather strength from this almighty God of theirs and they will forever be a thorn under Romans' armor."

Yes, that was it. The Romans found the solution to the "Jewish problem." Over the next sixty days, the Jews were told to back their belongings and leave the city and the land that Abraham said that their God had promised them. It was a sad time but after all the fighting the people were tired and there seemed to be no other recourse but to follow the Roman edict.

They were scattered to the north, to Europe, eventually to Italy, Russia and a dozen other countries. They were scattered to the south, to Africa Morocco, Algera and then to Spain. From there the Jewish people were scattered all over the globe—one might say, To the Four Corners.

2. The Scene Changes

In the two thousand years between the dismemberment of the Tribe of Judea and modern times, the world has seen an incalculable number of changes. But despite them, some characteristics have remained with us.

One of those is the Jewish people. I have often thought how Jews have continued to exist around the world, despite the terrible persecution. One day as I walked in the streets of Venice, I came upon a square that had a street sign which I was able to pronounce without knowing a word of Italian; The sign read GHETTO. It is from that little area that came that the concept of modern day segregation. Although anti-Semitism was not severe in the original Ghetto the concept of separating the Jews from the rest of the city, I believe, was the beginning of discrimination. Over the next five hundred years, there were ghettos established in Poland, in Russia, in Austria and Germany. There were so many that almost one-half the Jews in the world lived in them until beginning of twentieth-century. All over Europe there are Synagogues that were once the center of thriving Jewish communities which were given the name, Ghettos, derived from the original Italian word, "ghetto". But as I traveled around Europe I realized that most of these ghettos have little or no populations, most of them destroyed when the Nazis came to power. As our Jewish ancestors traveled around the world, not as tourists, but in order to survive against resistant persecution, they picked up certain customs and retained others.

So also, the use of the tallis has been a custom since the earliest days of Jewish antiquity, I took it very much for granted during most of my life. But just during the past few months there was an instance that brought the historic significance of the torah into focus.

During the Spanish Inquisition, the Jews began to pray in caves because the monarchy passed an edict forbidding prayer to the Jewish God. In order to keep their heads warm in those caves, they all began to wear yarmulkes. The wearing of the yarmulke became a custom and remains so for the past five hundred years.

3. The Tale Of The Tzitzis

During the last two months I have been writing a series of stories about my experience with the tallis used by many orthodox and conservative Jews and its fringes, called in Hebrew, tzitzis.

The story began in the section of Central Park called the conservatory Gardens or the Secret Gardens. It centers around a pretty little pond that has a statue of a young lady with a bird feeder and her brother playing a flute. The garden is so very beautiful with row upon row of plants designed to have blooms almost every time of the year from early April until the beginning of winter. I have visited this Gardens a score of times usually taking friends and relatives who come to New York and who want to see something very special. Everyone that I have taken to my secret garden has been so very impressed. The garden, because of its natural beauty, is often used by people getting married.

About two months ago I saw a beautiful African American bride dressed in a long white wedding gown emerge from a thirty-foot long limousine. A crowd of friends and relatives followed them into my special corner of the garden. In a while, very surprisingly, a lady friend who must have been twenty years her senior, joined her. At first I thought her friend was her mother, but when they kissed I knew this was very different. It was clear that these two women were living a very different lifestyle and were about to exchange vows in matrimony.

A tall well-dressed African American young man, dressed in a brilliant red African robe, officiated at the ceremony. I noticed that in addition to the robe, he was wearing a gorgeous Jewish prayer shawl which, in the Jewish religion, is called a tallis. I asked the minister if he knew what was inscribed on the tallis in Hebrew. When he said that he did not have a clue, I read to him the words in Hebrew. Then he asked me what was the significance of the special fringes in the four corners of the prayer shawl. I told him what I thought it meant—that the Jews had been scattered a throughout the world after the Romans captured Jerusalem. The fringes were to remind the Jews to return to their religious heritage. After I returned home I realized this was what I thought it meant but I was not sure.

So I sent out a series of e-mails asking friends if any of them knew for sure what those fringes meant. I received at least a half dozen answers. But only one of them was the very definitive conclusive answer.

As some of you may remember, the torah (the five books of Moses) had exactly 613 commandants. Now the question was how would the Jews remember such a very odd number. The next series of e-mails resulted in my finding out just how the name and number were derived.

Here was the answer: The easy part was the establishment of the number thirteen. The rabbis placed eight strings in each corner and placed five knots to secure the eight strings. So eight and five gave us the number thirteen. Now if they could only remember the number six hundred we would be home free, said the rabbis. So they very cleverly came up with a new word, tzitzis, that had the numerical value of 600.

So there you have it—600 plus 13 gives us the total number of commandments. Now everyone was satisfied with my explanation, except my son, Gary. When I told Gary about the answer, he wanted more information "how does the word tzitzis add up to the 600 you are telling us about. We all know that there are only twenty-two letters in the Jewish alphabet. How can you possibly get 600 from those 22 letters?"

It was then only a question of finding what the numerical values of the Hebrew letters actually were. The ancient Jews used the letters of the alphabet for numbers. Here are numbers, which were assigned the letters of their alphabet.

Starting with aleph, the first ten numbers were aleph. Beth, gimal, dalid, hay etc., etc. until they reached ten or yud. Then the next nine letters were used for the following numbers—20, 30, 40, 50, 60, 70, 80, 90, 100.

So now we have used up nineteen of the letters. The last three letters were given the numbers 200, 300, 400. The highest number the ancient Hebrews thought existed was 400.

So the word tzitzis was established to get to a total of 600 as follows: 90 (Tzadi) plus 10 (yud) plus 90 (Tzadi) plus 10 (yud) plus 400 ("Taf or saf", last letter of the alphabet). gives us the total of 600. The number 600 should have then been pronounced Taf-zadak—yad,-zadik—yad (400 plus 90 plus 10 plus 90 plus 10) but some how was shortened to 'tzitzis' The reason it was not Taf hok-hok (400 plus 100 plus 100) I have not found.

Clever those ancient rabbis, don't you think? But they didn't take into consideration that modern man would be too preoccupied with lottery numbers and poker games so that they would forget the origination of the development of the very word which was to remind us of the commandments which we were supposed to remember.

Secret Garden in Central Park, NYC,

GREECE

4. Costa's Magical Spirit

I found that the representatives we chose often led very interesting and exciting lives in addition to selling military electronics. One of the most interesting was a man named Costa (last name intentionally omitted.) The first time I met him I saw his office walls were pictured with all sorts of ships. There were submarines, destroyers, freighters and lots more. He told me that he represented some of the biggest shipyards in Germany and he sold to the Greek government and Greek ship companies for years. Selling ships seemed to be very different from Radar Warning Receivers (RWR), so I asked him why he was interested in becoming associated with us. He said that he liked the challenge of selling RWRs to the Hellenic Air Force. I immediately took a liking to this very intellectual soft-spoken man with a gentle heart (which I would find out in subsequent years).

As soon as we met I got to know him as a man with tremendous caring and honest ways. His sweet smile won me over and I immediately trusted and respected him. I loved his precise English as well as his intellect.

One day he invited me to his home in the center of Athens. As I walked in I was as impressed by the home as I was by the man. The five-story house was on a hill near a beautiful Athenian Park. We walked in at the bottom level that had a modern kitchen and dining area. Then we arrived on the living level that really shocked me. In the center of the living room was a huge grand piano. Around it was a dozen or so chairs where his audiences would listen to musical recitals. Costa would invite and entertain celebrities from all over the world to his home in Athens. I was very impressed. He was truly a man of art and culture. Then I was treated to another surprise.

As I sat in one of the living room chairs, Costa went over to the piano, sat at the bench, and suddenly his fingers began to fly across the keys. I said to him, "I never knew you played the piano."

Costa ceased for a moment to tell his story. He told us that he never played the piano in his life. He was almost seventy, when one day he just sat down at the piano and began to play like nothing he had ever heard himself. He just played on and on. His fingers glided across the keys and before he knew it he was playing as if he were a virtuoso.

Over the years as we sold many items to the Hellenic Air Force, Costa worked very hard to keep up our reputation with our customers. But he just maintained a small unobtrusive office with a one very hard working secretary. She was wonderfully efficient and kept his office in great condition. With her, Costa did not need anyone else. She was as sweet and nice as Costa.

The first time I walked into her office, on her desk was a single picture of her daughter who must have been ten years old at the time. From time to time when I visited Athens I would ask her about her daughter who must have been going to high school by then. As we worked with them during the 1980's either Jim Adams or I would always inquire about the secretary's daughter. Then one day Jim, (after coming back from over fifty trips to Athens) gave me the bad news that Costa's secretary was diagnosed with cancer. I immediately thought of her very pretty daughter whose picture always sat on her desk. Over the next months Jim told me how Costa was taking care of all his secretary's bills. But, despite all efforts, one day I received word that his secretary died.

A few months later I heard from Jim that Costa was paying all the college tuition for that little girl whose picture I could still visualize on the desk of an adoring mother and an efficient secretary. In a poor country like Greece that girl would have never gone to college without Costa's help. He always was there to share his good fortune working out of a little office in a three-story walkup in the old section of Athens.

Good deeds find their way even into little corners of little offices. Costa's piano playing was magic but so was the magic of his good deeds.

5. The Problem with Sailing the Aegean

The first cruise that most Americans take is in the Caribbean Sea with ports of call such as Jamaica, the Virgin Islands, or the Bahamas. They come away with great memories of fun in the sun and all that.

But Lila and I started our cruising activities in a very different part of the world. In the late 70s, we sailed from Piraeus, the port of Athens on a bright sunny day to spend one week in the Aegean Sea. The first island, Mycanos, that we reached has become one of my favorites on the planet. Our ship, the Stellar Solaris, anchored off shore and lowered the tenders for our first experience in going ashore by the use of these functional little boats. They run back and forth from ship to shore like excited little kids in a schoolyard.

We walked off the tender to a beautiful little port town with dozens of brightly painted boats bobbing in the water. At the water's edge were local townsmen painting and overhauling fishing boats. It was a busy industrial port to be sure. Across the street were a score of souvenir shops selling all the usual tourist items. We quickly walked past them and up the first street away from the harbor to a very picturesque street with houses on either side that had beautifully painted doors and tiny little gardens to match. We loved the place from the first look. Intermixed between the homes there were shops that sold sweaters and other handmade items. The sales people were warm and friendly. One store keeper I met was a retired Hellenic Air Force colonel and when I told him that I was in Greece to sell equipment to "his Air Force", he was ecstatic. We talked like old friends until I became anxious to continue our journey so I bid him farewell. When we reached the end of town, we came upon the harbor which has the four windmills, the symbol of Mykonos. What a beautiful sight! We took so many pictures I was concerned that we would run out of film.

A little further along a dirt road we came upon a church, the back yard of which faced a tiny harbor that had dozens of little fishing boats owned by the locals. It was a hot summer day as I walked down the four steps to the water's edge. I took my shoes and socks off and just dove right in with my clothes on. I swam around the boats as Lila took more pictures of the scene. I came out of the water totally refreshed and we continued our walk around Mykonos. What a wonderful day on a wonderful Island!

The next day the Stellar Solaris took us to one of the most unusual islands in the Aegean. Santorini is more like one-half an island. About 50,000 years ago in the center of this island was a huge active volcano. When it erupted, the burning hot lava rolled down the side of the mountain and one half of the island sunk into the sea leaving the remainder shaped like a curved sickle. Some ancient travelers called what was sunk around Santorini, the subterranean Island of Atlantis, but no proof of it has ever been found. Our ship anchored in the middle of the curvature and again we took those helpful little tenders to the boat basin.

The third day brought us to one of the largest and most historic of the Aegean islands, Crete. From the harbor we boarded a tour bus to the center of the island to an historic archaeological site called Knossos. Four thousand years ago Knossos was a magnificent and classic culture. The people of the area were major traders and developers of that society. Both the Grecians and the Egyptians would go to the Island and trade their products. From the grape fields, wine was cultivated and sold to the Egyptians. From the Egyptian fields, cotton was grown and sold to the Greeks.

YUGOSLAVIA/ALBANIA:

6. The Death of Communism Along the Adriatic

On another trip in the late 80s, we had just left the island of Corfu, which is near the mainland of Greece and at the entrance to the Adriatic Sea. It is a beautiful island and we spent an hour walking along the shore finally reaching the tip. There is an old fort there that has now been turned into a marina with hundreds of small fishing boats. If we had any extra time we could have taken a boat ride around the island to see its beauty.

But Lo and Behold! Once again we were under pressure of the clock and we only had four hours in Corfu. So we found a little tavern and had some lunch. After lunch we walked around a little park where they have horse and buggies just like we have in Central Park. We hopped on one and took the buggy around the city to get the flavor of it before heading for the ship.

We were in the final throws of a wonderful trip called the Seven Seas cruise and the Adriatic was to be the last of the seven. Tomorrow we would be stopping at the incredibly beautiful harbor of Dubrovnik—the last city before Venice, the terminus of the two-week cruise.

I was looking forward to visiting Dubrovnik. It is an ancient city, and fortunately it had not been destroyed during World War II. (Sadly, even though Dubrovnik had not been touched during the big war, since we were there in 1995, I understand the city had been severely damaged in the civil war in 2001.)

We left the Island of Corfu not knowing what was ahead for us in Dubrovnik, but optimistically I looked forward to a great day in that crossroads city. That evening we had a formal dinner because it was the next to last night on board. The last night of most cruises is reserved for packing and getting ready for the next day's disembarkation. It had been a wonderful trip and everyone came to dinner in their fanciest outfits.

There were incredibly beautiful designs of ice carvings in the entrance to the dining room. There were whales, salmon, and so many other carvings. Everyone looked at them with the usual "Ohs" and "Ahs." They then had a score of tables with hors d'ouvres of every kind imaginable. Finally the dinner was served with a choice of lobster or steak. At dinner that evening when everyone was in such a great mood, the captain, stood up and gave us something else to be happy about. He informed us that our ship had been given clearance to make a four-hour stopover in Albania. He told us that the port of Sarana had only been opened for one month since the Communist government had been deposed. We were going to be the only third ship to land in an Albania port in recent times.

The next morning all four hundred of us were lined upon the embarkation deck to await the tenders. The ship was anchored about one mile outside of the harbor because the pier was not large enough to berth the S. S. Americana. Our ship had five tenders and that morning they lowered all of them so everyone who wanted to go on shore, would be accommodated. Because this was such a rare opportunity, just about every single one of us decided to go on shore.

It was a bright, cool morning as the tenders were lowered into the bay and we carefully walked down the gangplank to board them. About fifteen minutes later we arrived at the shore. We were curious to see the Albanians, but they were just as curious to observe us. Naturally, the first thing that Americans do is to open their camera cases and start shooting away. But not in Albania. As soon as I took my camera out of the case and raised it to shoulder height, two soldiers came over to me and waved their hands to stop me.

"No pictures." one said. I looked around quizzically, shrugged my shoulders and made it clear that I could see no reason why I should not take pictures. There was nothing but a beach area with people sitting on the sand, across the street from the beach. There were several six and eight story apartment houses in pretty run down condition. Out in the harbor were two small gunboats with .50 caliber machine guns mounted fore and aft. Without a word but still questioning their decision, it suddenly dawned on me why I could not take pictures. They, no doubt, did not want the rest of the world to see what poor condition their Navy was in. But the Navy was reflective of the condition of the rest of the country. It was as bad as the worst of third world countries. We boarded into very dilapidated school buses to drive to an ancient archeological site. As we passed farm after farm, one could see the plows being pulled by water buffaloes. Can you imagine, seeing a farmer walking behind a wooden plow being towed by a water buffalo at the end of the twentieth century? We could have been in the most primitive parts of China.

We finally arrived at the site and got off the bus to see the ancient partially excavated temple. There were kids playing at the river edge but when they saw us, they dropped what they were doing and came over to put their hands out. Everybody gave them a few coins. The most heart wrenching aspect of the scene was the condition of these kids. They were so emaciated; they looked as bad as the children we saw in the most run-down villages of East Africa. Their bodies were so thin you could see every single one of their ribs. What a pitiful sight!

On the way back we stopped at a local hotel, which was set up as a souvenir shop to sell whatever they could scrap together. It was obvious that their economy was on the brink of disaster. In the backyard of the hotel a local band and dance group put together a show for the entertainment of the tourists and to sell a few drinks.

At the end of the show we walked back to the tenders with the most vivid understanding of how disastrous communism really was. No newspaper article, lecture or picture book could possibly present the real-life view that we experienced.

TURKEY

7. Ancient Ephesus: Where East Meets West

To me Turkey is one of the most exciting lands in the Central part of ancient Europe. Long before Alexander the Great left Macedonia to conquer the Eastern world, scores of civilizations settled in what was known in that part of the world as the Fertile Crescent. Between 2000 B. C. and 1200 B. C., there were many settlements between the Tigris and Euphrates Rivers. There were the Hittites, the Assyrians, the Babylonians and the Philistines who lived for several thousand years in this area now called Asia Minor.

Along the coast of the Aegean Sea there were many cities that lived off the trade between East and West. Caravans traveled throughout Asia Minor and settlements were set up at the edge of the sea where ships would be loaded with spices, materials, fruits, and wines. The goods would wait at the harbors for ships to come and bring these valuables to countries such as Egypt, Crete, Athens, and Sparta. One of them was the very ancient fortress city called Troy. Around the period of 800 B. C. Homer wrote about the fall of this city by the ancient warriors of Sparta and Athens some five hundred years before. After its destruction, other cities were established along the Aegean coast.

Within the last two hundred years archeologists have been digging around this coastal area looking for Troy. In the process of digging around Asia Minor, one of the ancient cities discovered was Ephesus. Two thousand five hundred years ago this city was on the coast of the Aegean Sea. Now this city is about one half-hour ride to the Aegean Sea.

When we made our first trip to the Aegean Sea in the 1970's, I was surprised to realize that Ephesus is almost thirty miles from the seacoast. It amazed me that so much water had receded in the past 2500 years. Our ship landed at the rather modern port town of Kesudases and we boarded tour buses to visit Ephesus, that two millenniums ago had as many as twenty thousand inhabitants. Our first stop-off was the amphitheater, which has been excavated marvelously in the past one hundred years. We walked through row upon row of benches that must have seated over two thousand viewers. Here the ancient times Greeks laughed and cried to the plays of Aeschylus, Sophocles and Euripides, and all the other Greek playwrights of the time.

We continued down the ancient boulevard to the cultural center of this old city. In the middle of the square on the opposite side was a magnificent two-story library made of huge marble blocks each one weighing a ton or so. It was one of the first two story structures I had ever seen from ancient times. As we stood in front of this very impressive structure, our guide had us gather in front of an unusual spot on this street. He then had us look down to the ancient granite stone that must have recently been dug up. On the ground were two footprints carved into the stone. He explained to us that these prints told the ancient visitors from other lands where to find the brothel. It was most interesting to me that, men who wanted to know where the houses of "ill-repute" were located, and being rather shy about asking, could find their needs met without having to ask. With a smile our guide said that even in those days men would visit the library to get their educational needs met. Then walk down the street to have some other needs met.

From the center of the city we followed another excavated lane to a magnificent marble temple along with a score or more of resurrected homes. This must have been the wealthiest part of Ephesus where the homes of the important citizens were located. It was clear to us that Ephesus had been a very classy city twenty centuries ago. When we reached the end of this ancient city, we met our bus, which drove us in back to the seaport.

In Kesudus we had an hour or two to visit the bazaar portion of the city where, as in other parts of Turkey, there were many carpet shops. In front of one shop was a man selling beautiful handmade rugs. Before we knew it we were inside looking at some magnificent carpets spread out all around us. They were not big but very exquisitely made silk carpets like no others I had ever seen. I always have been fascinated by rugs from around the world. In our home we have carpets from Morocco, (see Lost and Found In Fez in my book Chinese Walking Stick), from China and even other parts of Turkey like Istanbul and Ankara.

But these rugs were something else. Our salesman gave us a lecture on the varieties of carpets available. He explained to us that the number of stitches sewn to the inch, determined its value. He showed us carpets that had 1200 stitches to the inch and others with as much as 1800 stitches to the inch. Every time I looked at one that I liked and he told me the price, I told him that it was much too much. I was always drawn to the most expensive ones, but I wanted them closer to the price of the least expensive ones.

We were at a financial standoff as Lila sat quietly by watching the negotiation come to a standstill. Finally when it was clear that we were at a complete impasse, she took the salesman over to the side and the two of them had a quiet conversation. She told him that I was a very stubborn man and that I was about to get up and walk out and once I would leave there would be no returning for me. So he had better become more flexible or he would have wasted his last two hours and there would be no sale. When he came back he did become more flexible and we did in fact get the carpet with the 1800 stitches to the inch for just a little more than the price of the 1200 stitches to the inch.

We rolled up our little treasure and before long we were back on the ship with our prize magic carpet. I think of the days thousands of years ago when the traders from the East met the West and of all those millions of items that must have been sold between those two worlds.

Now in our Manhattan apartment, every time I pass by that magnificent rug hanging on our hall I think of my wife's very clever negotiating technique. When I thank her for using her talents, she says, "It was not a technique, I think. In fact, you probably would have walked out without it if he had not come down in price. I smile as I touch this very smooth piece of silk and think that only I would know what I would have done.

8. Dinner in Ankara

The biggest European customer we had for Radar Warning Receivers was the Hellenic Air Force. In the late 1970's we closed a ten million dollar contract to put RWRs in their fighter aircraft. Now the Greeks and the Turks were two countries who had been at odds going back to the time that the Turks set the Acropolis on fire about six hundred years ago. Currently they have tensions about the Greek Islands that lay less than ten miles off the Turkish mainland. The Turks feel uncomfortable about having the Greek islands so close to their fortresses. The government of these islands have been held by Greek populations for hundreds of years and have no intentions to relinquish the islands, that have vast majorities of Greek populations, to Turkish rule.

Since the end of WWII the United States of America has been acting as an "honest broker" between the two nations. Over the years the USA has given military aid to each of them, but not enough for one to become vastly superior to the other. The basic purpose has been to keep both out of the hands of communism. When one country received fighter aircraft a few years later the other would get some aid to offset the strength of the other. Giving the Hellenic Air Force modern RWRs for their fighters meant that the Turks would certainly want comparable equipment. They especially wanted them for the new F-16's they were getting from General Dynamics.

In addition to my company, there was Litton Industries and Loral who were bidding for the RWR's in the late 1980's. Although we had won the Greek RWR contract we hoped to win the Turkish order as well. The only way to have a chance to win such an order was to have a well-connected representative (rep). We interviewed several companies who were totally involved with the Ankara scene. Finally we chose a company that although small, seemed to be very well contacted with the key Turkish Air Force General Staff. In order for myself to feel comfortable about their connection, I decided to visit Ankara myself and meet the key technical and operational staff.

Our Turkish rep, Jim Adams, Vice President of Marketing, and I spent almost a week there, meeting all the right people. I was very impressed that our new rep was indeed very well known, and knowledgeable about the RWR scene.

On the last day before leaving, the Turkish rep invited us for dinner, to one of the most prestigious restaurants in the capitol. He met us at our hotel and drove us to the restaurant. As the three of us walked in, our rep seemed to be on excellent relations with the owner because despite the crowds, we were immediately given a front row table.

We enjoyed a wonderful meal and great music from a first rate band. After we ate our dinner, the bandleader walked over and said something in Turkish to our rep and, I just assumed they were good friends. In a while, the bandleader stopped the dance music and said something in Turkish to the entire crowded restaurant to which the audience applauded loudly. Then to my surprise, our rep stood up, walked to the stage, sat down at the drums and started to play. He was just wonderful; he reminded me of Gene Krupa of my early jitterbug years. He played on and on, in a way I had never heard before. At last he finished his solo to a standing ovation. He quietly walked back to our table.

I said to him. "Boy, that was just great. I bet you played a lot in your early days?" After awhile and with some prodding, he modestly told us that he had his own band for many years and in those days, he was the Number One drummer in Turkey! I asked him "How did you get into the rep business?" He told me that his father was very well connected with the Air Force but after he died, his son had to decide whether to follow his music career or his father footsteps. With a tear in his eye, he said, "I left the music field in favor of my father's business."

I thought to myself what a difficult decision he must have had to make. What a struggle to chose between a career that he worked so hard to develop, or follow the business his father had worked a lifetime to build up. Yes, indeed, learning to play the drums must have been hard, but making such lifetime decisions are often much harder.

I left the restaurant with a much better understanding of our new rep and his life struggles, in addition to enjoying a great Turkish dinner.

9. Turkey: Downhill

One of the most exciting cities that we have ever visited is Istanbul. Of course everyone knows that it is in Turkey, but few know that it lies in two continents, Europe and Asia. It is an ancient city first named Istanbul than was changed to Constantinople and then changed back again to Istanbul.

Our ship docked along the Bosporus Sea on the Asian side. As we disembarked there was a crew member telling us to turn left and not go to the right. Apparently on the right side of the pier there was a very nasty neighborhood.

We did as we were told and found ourselves in a safe and exciting section of this wonderful city. The area was full of pushcarts with hustling salesmen selling fresh fish wrapped in newspaper to the workers on their way home. As we walked along the Bosporus Sea we saw dozens of ferries taking these workers to their homes in Europe from their working district in Asia. It seemed curious to me to work in one continent of our planet and live in another one. But I am sure these people never give it a thought, any more than Americans living in New Jersey and working in New York.

We left the piers and headed in the direction of the mosque and minarets where the tourists assembled to see some of these magnificent sights. We passed by most of the high-pressure salesmen and visited the mosques along the Bosporus especially the Sophia Mosque. The Sophia with its gold-domed roof and the four pointed minarets at each corner is absolutely spectacular. The shear wealth and beauty of these mosques, lived in by the sultans of bygone days, is extremely impressive.

Outside of the Sophia were young men who stayed there to capture the tourists and drag them to the grand bazaar. They spoke just enough English to ask the only question they seemed to know: Wh're you from? Chicago? Wh're you from? New York?" They are told at their shops to open any conversation with tourists with such a query because they assume every tourist is from the United States. After hearing that line of questioning from these aggressive young men you learn to avoid them. Their goal is to get you down to the bazaar section of the city where there are hundreds of shops selling mostly rugs. These men get a commission for every tourist they bring into their boss's shop.

After we did the usual sightseeing of Mosques and Minarets we did go down to the bazaar because one has not visited Istanbul until one visits the Grand Bazaar. The bazaar is so huge it stretches for several miles around the center of Istanbul and there are over one thousand shops down the many narrow covered streets. It is not the smelly and dirty bazaar like the old cities of Fez and Casablanca but, nevertheless, there is the intensity and high-pressure salesmanship of those old madinas. Outside each shop are the usual young men trying to draw you in. "Where are you from, New York?. My uncle lives there? Come see our carpets? Come see our carpets. Best prices in the bazaar"

Instead of taking the typical guided tour around the city we hired a local cab driver who assured us he spoke English. He drove us all around both the European and Asian sides of the city. In addition to the many ferries across the Bosporus there was a new and beautiful high suspension bridge. Our guide drove us to the modern city where all the wealthy business people live. On the way back across the bridge we experienced some real excitement.

Our tour guide drove an American old car that obviously was very uneconomical on fuel. Another fact that he told us was gasoline is very expensive in Turkey. I believe it was over the equivalent of $4.00 per gallon in the early nineteen-nineties. His car used up a significant amount of fuel going up the suspension bridge. In order to make up for it, we were astounded to watch as the driver turned off his engine at the top of the bridge and let his car coast without using his brakes all the way down the opposite side, and, for what seemed to be miles, finally reaching the end of the bridge. Then to get the maximum benefit he let the car free wheel, and we just sped down the highway for many minutes. It was an exciting ride with the windows open, because he had no air conditioning, and it gave me the feeling of a roller coaster ride in Coney Island. He smiled a toothless smile to tell us how much he was saving in fuel by turning off his engine and free-wheeling it down the highway at over one-hundred–twenty kilometers and hour. We were dumbfounded.

After a while he turned the engine on and the excitement was over. I am not sure just how many sections of Istanbul we saw that day but I surely remember the wild ride down the Bosporus suspension bridge.

EGYPT

10. The Gift of the Nile

Joe and I spent twelve exciting days in Egypt and all I have written about it so far in my first book, "The Chinese Walking Stick", was getting around in a wheel chair. A country that is as exciting as Egypt deserves more than that, so here is a tale of this ancient land.

Twenty four hundred years ago a famous Greek historian, Heroditus, decided to take a trip to Egypt because even in those days it was the place to visit. When he returned to Athens he wrote about the country and coined the phase that has lasted for these twenty-four centuries, "Egypt is the Gift of the Nile". Of course what Heroditus meant is that there would be no Egypt without the Nile and the Nile makes Egypt possible. After traveling throughout the country I would agree that without the Nile Egypt would be nothing more than a desert wasteland. The best way to visualize the country is in its center at the more modern city of Aswan. Joe and I stayed in a modern hotel in Aswan. In the afternoon we sat in wonderful little garden and watched the feluccas, sailing boats, plying up and down the Nile. It was such a calming and relaxing sight that one would never believe that a few hundred miles north there are nineteen million people crowded into the city of Cairo. I will be talking about it in a while but for now let's enjoy the wonderful serenity of Aswan.

Here in Aswan we were not living the Egypt of the pharaohs or the modern day tensions, but just enjoying the sunshine and the beauty of it all. In the early evening we walked down to the boat basin and hired a felucca and a pair of drivers and went out into the Nile River for a sailing trip so peaceful and relaxing, I will never forget it. There were about a dozen such feluccas with their tall white sails fluttering in the breeze and silently going up and down the river. On the east side was a natural preserve, which was developed by a wealthy philanthropist. In the sky were hundreds of birds that made this little park, their home. We watched the birds peacefully sitting in the trees that no doubt had been transplanted from the more tropical parts of central Africa.

The amazing part of the entire scene is the unbelievable transformation from the beauty and serenity of the park-like setting surrounding the Nile compared with the stark nothingness just a couple of hundred feet on either side. As one looks just a short distance to either side of the Nile you see the incredible comparison from the green of the preserve to the absolutely stark nothingness of the beige-colored Sahara desert.

Our felucca bobbed calmly through the Nile, while all around were families in other feluccas enjoying an evening on their river. In the middle of the river was an Island that had one of the most magnificent hotels in Egypt. The hotel, the Oberie, had its own passenger vessel of the same name, which was docked at the island. The tourists would sail up the river and then have a three-day stay at their hotel. Our boat and about fifty others were docked up river closer to the Aswan dam. Almost all the tourists who came to Egypt would also take a cruise on the Nile. It is the elegance and tranquility part of the trip. The steam ships stopped off at three temples, which gave us much history of the ancient pharaohs.

One of the most interesting places I remember was the marble quarry about fifty miles south of Luxor. In Luxor we saw the obelisk, which stands in front of the main temple. We were then told how these obelisks were removed in one piece from the bowels of the earth. When we came to the quarry there was still one obelisk, which had never been taken from the earth because it developed a small crack and the ancient workers realized it would not survive the removal. Of course this now gave us the opportunity to see how they take the stone out of the ground Apparently they would use hammers and chisels to crack all along the entire surface. But the most difficult was cutting along the bottom. It is believed that they froze the water, which would then expand and crack the stone all along the hundred-foot bottom of this huge stone. Then with ropes and skids they would slide the huge obelisk down to the edge of the Nile and place two of them, one on each side, of a huge raft and sail it down to the temple at Luxor.

One of the most magnificent of all the temples is the one called Abu Simbel. It is much farther south than the cities of Luxor or Karnac. It is lower than the second cataract (Falls). The temple was originally at the level of the Nile that was much lower than the present day level of Lake Nasser, and in the 1960's, had to be moved 190 feet up when the Aswan Dam was built and the lake behind it was flooded. The two temples built into the side of a mountain had to be cut into thousands of sandstone blocks to be saved from the rising waters of the lake. It must have been a tremendously difficult job to build the temple over three thousand years ago and almost as difficult to move it in the last forty years. Joe and I flew down to Abu Simbel one clear day and boarded buses to the edge of the Lake Nasser. As we left the bus, I got into the wheelchair and Joe pushed me for about two hundred yards until the ground got so bumpy that it was impossible to go any further. But I was not going to miss this sight. I had to get out of the wheelchair and use a cane the rest of the way. Then at last we were standing in front of these huge temples with the statues of Ramses ll and his wife, Nefertari, built some thirty-two hundred years ago during his sixty-six year reign. They were just magnificent beyond compare. After standing transfixed at the beauty of these figures, we walked into the darkened inner court (Hypostyle Hall) behind the statues. On the wall facing the front entrance were four smaller statues. Three were gods and the fourth, of course, was Ramses ll, himself. They were arranged so that at a certain day of the year and at a time when the sun reached a location in its orbit across the sky, it would shine straight through the entrance into the back of the Temple and directly on the face of Ramses, The Magnificent. Amazingly, as Joe and I approached the four statues, we saw Ramses' face suddenly LIGHT UP. What a sight! There we were; at the right place and the proper time, to see the sun shine on the face of this most impressive of Pharaohs. It was just awesome.

After leaving Abu Simbel, we spent two days in Cairo visiting the Museum and sightseeing around the city. The one very impressive and rather weird scene was the city cemetery. The cemetery is used by many families as a place to live. It was very difficult to get used to the fact that families with little kids were living in this cemetery. We stood on the side of the cemetery watching the children running around the gravestones playing hide and seek. The city is so crowded that even cemeteries are used for living space. What a country and what a city.

As we arrived in Cairo we met our new guide, a young man in his thirties. Abdullah was married and he and his wife had a ten-year-old daughter. After we became friendly, he confided in us that he was having a family problem that was very distressing to him. He told us that his wife and his mother-in-law were insisting that his daughter be circumcised. It is a Moslem ritual that is both painful and affects a woman's sexual life. It was surprising to both Joe and I that his wife would be so traditional whereas he was much more modern about the action. Hearing his interpersonal tale was the first time I had ever heard a Moslem talk so openly about this subject. All we could do was listen and think how different their world is from ours.

Ramses ll & God Osiris at Abu Simbel, Egypt

Ramses ll & Queen Nefertari at Abu Simbel, Egypt,

BULGARIA

11. A Funny Thing Happened On The Way To Bulgaria.

One of my favorite sea voyages in the early 90s was called the Seven Seas Cruise. It was named that for the obvious reason that our ship sailed the seven original seas: the Ligonian, Tyrrhenian, Mediterranean, Adriatic, Ionian, Sea of Marmara, and the Black Sea. In ancient times the entire world was considered to be centered around these seas. To take a trip through them seemed very romantic and adventurous even though we now know that that the seven seas are but a small fraction of planet Earth.

The cruise started off in Genoa, Italy and then stopped at Sorrento, Piraeus, Istanbul, Nessebur, Odessa, Yalta, Corfu, Dubrovnik, Yugoslavia and then concluded in Venice. As I read the brochure, I knew that this was going to be a great trip—I was not disappointed.

The first port was Sorrento in the Bay of Naples. Lila and I had been there about ten years before when we took a boat to Capri, walked around the hills and sailed into the cave of the Blue Lagoon. This time we decided to pass up Capri and strolled the harbor of Sorrento watching the sailors readying the fishing boats for the season. The many little ports around Sorrento are very colorful and we had a great time just perusing the harbor. It is something that I could not do now, but I am very glad that I had the opportunity to do it then.

The next port of call was Piraeus, the port city of Athens. Since we had been to Athens many times before we just stayed around the port. Coincidentally, the Defense Electronics Show was being held at the time our ship entered the port and even more coincidentally, our ship was docked next to the Exhibition Hall. So we had the opportunity to visit with many of my old friends who were exhibiting at the show. We went to lunch with Elias Evangelou and his wife, Jenny, and Dotty Adams, Jim's wife, and several other friends including Ron Myer, our Program Manager, from my General Instrument days. After lunch I remember going back to the Exhibition Hall and walking around like a tourist instead of an exhibitor. It was a memorable day indeed.

We sailed from Piraeus to Istanbul through the Dardanelles and stopped off at the famous memorial at Gallipoli where the Turks and the Aussies had a vicious battle during WW1. The Australians were severely beaten losing many thousands of soldiers. It was the worst defeat of the war for the Allies. The Turks have built a Memorial for the gallant soldiers of both sides who died there.

We continued the cruise in a more somber mode for several hours but then landed at Istanbul for a day of adventure and excitement.

Istanbul is a very vibrant city. it is built on both continents, Europe and Asia. People scurry from one continent to the other, in the same way we would go from Brooklyn to Manhattan in the daily rush hour. In Istanbul, however, there are dozens of ferries shuttling the citizens from home to work each day. At about five in the evening there is a mad dash for the ferries and the most exciting time to be at the piers. Alongside the ferries are lots of fishing boats that come in just in time to sell their freshly caught hauls. The commuter stops off on the way to his ferry to buy a fresh fish for his nightly meal.

It was with great excitement that I watched them rush down to the harbor, hustle over to the fishing boat, negotiate with the fisherman, grab their fish wrapped in a sheet of newspaper and run off to their ferry in a matter of minutes. Most of the other tourists were at the Blue Mosque or the Hagia Sophia Mosque, the largest Mosque in the world, but Lila and I had done that before, so this trip was to just sit and watch the Turks in their daily routine. To me it was just as exciting as seeing the Mosque, for this was the living Turkey. From the harbor we went to the Grand Bazaar and, as usual, it was crowded with tourists and hawkers. In Istanbul the hawkers are extremely obnoxious. They just do not let you alone. Their perennial questions are" "Where are you from? "or "are you from Chicago?, I have an Uncle there". If you answer, they keep on badgering you to go with them to their kiosk, to buy a rug or a scarf or a whatever.

I believe that most people, especially Americans, do not appreciate this form of salesmanship and they would buy more if they were not pressured. But nevertheless we did buy a beautiful oriental rug that hangs on our wall in our New York apartment. Each time I go by, I touch it and feel its elegant softness and remember our trip to Turkey with a smile.

After leaving the Bosporus we entered into the Black Sea and headed north along the Bulgarian coast. Our first stop in this ocean sized inland body of water called the Black Sea, was Nessabur. We walked from the port to a sandy resort beach to watch the locales enjoying their summer holiday. The beach was crowded with hundreds and hundreds of families. It could have been Jones Beach or Jacob Riis Park.

As we walked among the Bulgars, they were all jabbering in a tongue entirely unfamiliar to us. What was familiar to us were the bumper cars going around in circular track just like the ones in Coney Island. The laughing children also were so familiar to me. At that moment I suddenly realized that laughing in any language is all the same. We walked back to the ship clicking away with our cameras. It was a hot summer day on the beach in Bulgaria. Probably our first and last visit to that nondescript country on the Black Sea and yet I still remember that little beach with those laughing kids.

UKRAINE

12. A Gift For Odessa

We had boarded the S. S. Americana in Genoa, Italy and were traveling east as did Alexander the Great twenty-five hundred years ago. We first visited Portofino, a sophisticated little harbor where the rich and richer anchor their one hundred foot yachts. Then sailed through the Tyrolean, Mediterranean, Aegean, Ionian Seas and the Sea of Marmora edging the coast of Turkey and stopping off for a day at the ancient city of Istanbul (originally called Constantinople), which straddles the continents of Europe and Asia.

At last we arrived at the Black Sea that is surrounded by five historic countries: Turkey, Romania, Bulgaria, Russia and the Ukraine. The night before our ship arrived at the Ukrainian port of Odessa, we met a Jewish couple in the dining room from Montreal, Canada. They told us that they were looking forward to their visit to Odessa because they brought about one dozen prayer books to donate to any temple which may still exist in this ancient city. They explained to us that the Friday before they left for Europe their rabbi gave them the prayer books to donate to any synagogue that they may visit. They asked us if we wanted to join them in a search for such a temple. I said, that since we had not signed up for a formal tour, it would be a good idea to just wander around and see what we could find.

The next morning we met our new friends at the wharf and started to make our plans for the day. Then suddenly from out of the crowd came a tall thin Ukrainian man walking with a young preteen girl. He came up to me and introduced himself as Carl and told us that he expected to be immigrating to the USA in a few months. He said that he would like to refresh his English so would I mind if we had a short conversation in my language. Among other things he told us that he was a sonar engineer and he hoped to resettle in Boston and find a job there. I could not believe the coincidence. Here he meets me, the manager of a sonar engineering facility just outside of Boston.

When I told him these facts, he was just thrilled. As we talked our new Canadian friends introduced themselves and the coincidence grew stronger. The couple from Canada explained their mission to find a synagogue. Carl then told us that he was Jewish and that he had a Temple to which he could drive us where they could donate their prayer books. He continued to talk to us in English.

"I am trying improve my English since we will be leaving for the United States soon. We are one of the few Jewish families remaining in Odessa," he said. He explained that the reason for moving was because his sixteen-year-old son had been having problems with anti-semitism in his high school. Then, as an afterthought, he told us he brought his daughter to the port because he thought people like ourselves would treat his request to speak English more seriously if he had his daughter with him.

It had turned out to be a very interesting day and I often wonder if Carl ever got to America and what happened to him. It often intrigues me how many strangers I have met during my travels and their individual personalities remain with me. In addition to viewing the sights is such an important reason to travel.

13. Yalta: Remembering FDR

We left Odessa after a wonderful day and traveled all night to arrive in Yalta the next morning. Yalta is a beautiful resort city at the tip of the Crimea peninsular. We signed up for a tour to the mansion where in 1944, Roosevelt, Churchill and Stalin met to plan a world of peace after the victory in World War II was secure.

We rode for about one hour through the countryside. All throughout the area were magnificent homes that belonged to Russian aristocracy before the communist revolution in 1917. I had never realized that there were so many rich Russians during that period. In our history books we were told that the Royal Family had all the money. I learned on that trip after seeing hundreds of mansions along the Yalta coastline that there were indeed many wealthy families. The homes reminded me of Newport, Rhode Island or Bar Harbor, Maine. Our guide told us that after the Russian revolution the homes were taken over by the new communist leaders—so much for equality of the masses under communism. Some estates were used by the labor parties as summer vacation homes for their workers, but gradually they became the homes of the communist leaders.

We arrived at the mansion where the world leaders met. We walked around it in awe. It was a huge estate overlooking the Black Sea, somewhat like Washington's Mount Vernon.

We stood at the very site were they met. In the hall before the conference room were many pictures commemorating the historic meeting. As we looked at a picture of the three statesmen, a young woman, in her twenties, turned to her friend and asked a question that I have never forgotten, "Which one is Roosevelt?" Her friend, too, was uncertain and I, pointing to Roosevelt, said, "This one was our president." I found it hard to believe that two American women would not know the face of the most famous president of the twentieth century. But then I reasoned that when I was her age I probably would not have known the name of the president fifty years back. Time certainly has a way of erasing historical memories.

We stopped off at several other mansions and then returned to the center of the city to shop for souvenirs. In the evening we started our return cruise through the Black Sea, the Bosporus and the Dardanelles heading for the Greek Island of Corfu.

We traveled the Corinthian Canal early the next morning and found it spectacular. It was amazing to me how the Greek engineers were able to cut their way through a mountain to construct this canal. So much is talked about the Suez and Panama Canals, but very few people even heard of the Corinthian Canal. On the deck of the Royal Princess we took dozens of pictures of what, I thought, was a very impressive sight.

Few hours later we disembarked at Corfu to walk around this very pretty island. Lila and I took a ride in a horse and buggy like the ones in Central Park. Even though we live some of the time in New York City, we never have rode a horse and buggy. Afterwards we sat at the beach and took in the breezes of the beautiful Adriatic.

We took a bus tour throughout out the countryside that consisted mostly of little farms growing rice. We stared in complete surprise to see water Buffalo pulling their plows just like we saw in China a decade ago. What a backward country Albania was!

But even more pitiful were the young boys playing along the roadside. You could see their ribs showing through their skin tight bodies. They looked terribly undernourished. In awhile our bus stopped off at an ancient ruin from the days of Greek supremacy. Near the ruins was a river that emptied out to the Adriatic. Another surprise was the ferryboat going across it. It was more like a raft with wooden slates for sides. It propelled across by three men pulling on a rope stretched across the river. The ferry gradually moved to the opposite side. It reminded me of the flat boats that I read about in the Tom Sawyer and Huckleberry Finn days. Maybe, the boys hanging around the ferry piers were Albania's Tom and Huck.

After exploring the Greek ruins we headed back to the beach of the little city of Saranda. The tour guide took us to a hotel and for a couple of dollars we got to see an Albanian dance group. They were dressed in red costumes and the dances were somewhat like the Russian acrobatic dancers and not half bad. A surprising fact was that they didn't have many souvenirs to sell. The few things they did have for sale had labels reading,"made in China"(not modern China, but the 1930's kind).

We walked along the seawall watching the kids swimming in the surf. Swimming everywhere seems to be their fun pastime.

We embarked by tenders after a very busy day and set sail for Dubrovnik, our last port. In the morning we walked the little old streets of this famous resort town. We found the last remaining synagogue, and Lila and I along with about twenty of our group who were Jewish, went inside to pay our respects. It was very small and the biemer was in the middle of the sanctuary, not in the end. Before the Holocaust there were thousands of Jews in this area but now sadly there are just a handful. This is true in almost every city in Europe. We sat in the little synagogue for several minutes trying to think how a tragedy as horrendous as the Holocaust could have possibly taken place. After a while, I stepped out of the darkened schule to the bright sunlight of the streets of Dubrovnik with a lump in my throat and tears in my eyes.

This, of course, was before the ethnic fighting destroyed the beautiful city. They, too, had a form of Holocaust but on a much smaller scale. It just amazed me how people could do such terrible destruction to one another. I tried to shake off these unbelievable thoughts.

We walked into farmers market that had dozens of little stalls selling local produce to the citizens of Dubrovnik. I love to take pictures of the elderly men and women with wrinkled faces, sitting behind their tables and quietly waiting for someone to buy something. At their feet are typically little grandkids playing with their toys, oblivious to their surroundings like kids anywhere. What a peaceful idyllic setting.

In the late afternoon, we boarded our ship to complete the cruise now headed toward the wondrous water city of Venice.

Lila and I have visited the canals of Venice several times before and I have written about that city on other occasions.

We have taken about a dozen cruises and each one has had its own special remembrances but there are not many as great as the Seven Seas.

RUSSIA

14. Russian Rules and Regulations

It was during the cold war in the early 1980s when Lila and I first landed in St. Petersburg (Leningrad) from the Norwegian liner S. S. Americana. We were given a series of scares that made us feel as though we might end up in a Soviet prison if we did not do everything according to their very strict laws. For example according to the U. S. S. R. regulations everyone had to declare the exact amount of currency of all nationalities that each traveler was bringing into their country. We were given a form that required us to fill out the exact amount of money in our possession.

Now Lila often took more money to a port city than she even told me she was taking. She liked to buy lots of gifts for herself and others without having to account for every cent. In this case after getting the Russian declaration and the thought of a prison sentence, she decided to list every dollar that she had in her possession. I guess that she had rather have my annoyance for spending so much money than the Russian anger for not being accurate about her funds. I laughed to think I was the lesser of two evils.

One of the most insecure feelings a person has about landing in Russia is their taking away your passport. I had this concern, as we walked off the gangplank and a Russian uniformed officer put out his large hand and said, "Passport, Please." I gave it to him. Of course this now meant that we had to walk around the city without our passports, and that is such a scary feeling. We had to remain with our escorted group or else we would get into severe trouble. Every place we visited, we were transported in buses that were followed by black unmarked cars that were obviously driven by KGB members. They made it very apparent to us that we were kept under close surveillance.

We were taken to three locations on the first day. The first place was a huge shopping mall because the Russian authorities know that Americans love to shop (and because the Russians wanted our dollars). You were given Russian rubles in exchange for our dollars, but once you had them you could not get your dollars back. The typical items that everyone bought were the Russian "grandmother dolls", that fit one inside the other. The usual doll had from six to ten of those wooden 'mother dolls' one within each other. They were hugely over–priced, like everything else was in St Petersberg. The other items that were for sale, beside post cards and postage stamps were embroidered napkins, table cloths and aprons of the cheapest quality. As we walked around the mall I realized that everything was of very poor quality. In those days Russian workmanship was on the par with India and much worse than China. We were not permitted to visit any other stores outside of the mall. It was a little like a two-hour prison sentence. Since we could not get our dollars back and most of us exchanged our dollars for too many rubles, we finally spent all our Russian money for the junk on sale. After our "shopping spree" we were herded back on buses and went off to a mass restaurant and luncheon show. We pulled up to a gigantic building somewhat like the mall and outside were thirty or forty buses with other tourists going into this mass production kind of restaurant. We were reminded of our bus number so we would not get lost especially after our vodka-loaded meal. The huge room had long straight tables and you sat at your numbered table that had just enough seats for our busload. Everything was well organized.

The meal started with a drop of caviar on a little corrugated cracker. Then you were served a bowl of hot red borscht with a boiled potato. Following that came the main dish of meat and more potatoes. Some where between the borscht and the meat came entertainment. There were female dancers followed by Red Army soldiers, who were really pretty good. The one problem that was not well handled was going to the rest rooms. There were not enough rooms and many people had to wait on line. This confused the KGB who did not know whether to stay at the dining room tables or stand in front of the ladies and men's room.

As I went to the men's room, I passed by a KGB man dressed in a dark suit but he must have tasted some of the vodka because he smelled like it. The only contact we had with the everyday Russian was looking out of the dining room windows and seeing women with baby carriages or if the children were older they would be walking alongside their mothers. The little girls wore very long unstylish dresses just like their mothers.

One other slight contact we had was when we saw the people on the streets standing in from of a newspaper stand, reading the newspaper. Apparently paper was so expensive that the average man-on-the-street could not buy a paper but had to read it from a bulletin board. Then the final Russian contact was to see the people waiting on line to buy their daily bread. We could see that there was very little bread in the shops and many more people wanting to buy.

The last activity was an evening entertainment in the St. Petersburg theatre. Again it was the usual but wonderful Russian dancers. They seem to be able to leap all over the stage. But after you have seen one, it seems you have seen them all. Some leap higher and some are more graceful, others try to be comical. But I was not very impressed with Russian dancers.

The next day was dedicated to visits to Hermitages, one of the most beautiful museums in all of Europe. That was worthwhile.

POLAND

15. Forever Amber

Lila and I had just left St. Petersburg where we experienced the control and intensity of living in a communist country, even though it was only for a few days. Now we were on our way to Poland that was still under the pressure of communism. The day before we arrived, we were given strict instructions to bring in no more than $20.00 into the country. Obviously, we imagined Poland to be rigid like Russia, when it came to following rules and regulations. In Russia the KGB followed us everywhere we went.

There was no way that we were going to take any chances. When the rules said bring in no more than $20.00 Lila and I were not going to bring in a penny more than $20.00. I even took out my extra change to be sure I was absolutely within the $20.00 rule. I knew that Lila would have loved to buy a lot of amber jewelry and bring them back to the family members, but I urged her to keep within the rule.

The ship carried about four hundred passengers and I bet that every one of us followed the rule. But of course there were other tourists in Poland beside the ones on ships. And if I had thought it over, I would have realized that they had to have more than $20.00 in their possession. As we walked through the little city of Gdansk we came upon a center of shopping and jewelry markets. There were dozens of people buying jewelry and especially amber in many of these shops.

Amber is mined throughout the hills of Poland and probably more amber is mined in Poland than anywhere else in the world.

So naturally, Poland has become the major semi-precious jewelry market throughout Europe. Lila looked at all the great bargains in amber and was absolutely disheartened. She would have loved to buy much more amber. She borrowed my $20.00 and the twenty of another passenger. But she still felt as though this once-in-a-lifetime opportunity to get great bargains in amber would never happen again. To get such great amber at those prices was gone forever. When we came back to the ship we discussed it with members of the crew and found that they often brought in many hundreds of dollars in Amber and there was never a problem. But now our opportunities to buy more amber were gone forever.

2

Caesar's Conquests

FRANCE

1. The Mediterrean Surprise

Hidden between the major port cities of Toulon and Marseilles is a tiny fishing village of Cassis. Joe, my traveling companion and I were attracted to it when I read about its interesting geological formation just a mile or two to its west.

During my travels around the world I have encountered a wide variety of geological formations. All over this globe of ours there are many irregularities which give an observer exciting views about the wonders of planet earth. In New Zealand, the coastal bays explored in the 17th century by Captain James Cook intrigued Lila and me. We took a daylong boat trip down the Milford Sound to view its beautiful Bridal Falls. Behind a magnificent one hundred foot cascade of water, is a fissure in the earth's mantle caused by earthquakes that shook the Milford Sound area at the rate of one a day. Another geological formation of interest was found north of the quaint city of Bergen, Norway. I was attracted to the huge fjords which go deep inland for scores of miles along its magnificent coast.

In Iceland, we experienced the tremendous contrast between the heat of a geyser pouring forth sulfur from the center of the earth to the freezing cold glacier less than one mile apart. In Chile and Alaska one marvels at the mountainous glaciers receding or advancing with the worlds changing temperatures. Then in the city of Kunming in the far-off China there are magnificent petrified stone mountains that were once under the ocean but now are one thousand miles from the sea.

In our own country the magnificent volcano we all know as Mount St Helens reminds us regularly of the awe and might of the earths interior. During my professional career we developed a sophisticated electronic system which helped discover the earths tectonic plates.

The more I travel around our earth, the more I observe such varieties of geological beauty. When I think I have seen them all, another interesting phenomenon makes me realize once again how beautiful and varied is our little planet.

Now, to prove the point, a mile or two from this little fishing village, I came upon another formation I had never heard of before. We all know that the Mediterranean coast is recognized for its beaches, little harbors and deltas, but it is also where we discovered the coastal surprise called Calanques (rhymes with banks). Sitting in our hotel room in the city of Aix en Provence, I read a brochure with an unusual advertisement: BE SURE TO SEE THE CALANQUES. The picture accompanying the ad was a beautiful white cliff behind a picturesque harbor.

"What's this?" I asked Joe, my travel companion. "Just what are the Calanques?" Joe shrugged his shoulders. "Never heard of them," he said. Joe and I were at the beginning of our two-week travel experience from Marseilles to Toulouse. But I decided we would take a day to find out.

One hundred million years ago this part of the France was deep under water. Over many millenniums, limestone cliffs were formed from flowing rivers where the water receded to etch away these beautiful limestone cliffs. This is somewhat similar to the formation of the Grand Canyon in Arizona. Just as the Grand Canyon cliffs were once under the Colorado River, so the Calanques were under the Mediterranean Sea. The limestone cliffs form a magnificent part of the coast adjacent to the little port town of Cassis. There are miles of these rocky limestone cliffs that line the many tiny inlets. Those little tiny harbors were wonderful resting places for Julius Caesar and his legions as they traveled from Rome to Spain during their invasion of that country. We arrived from Aix en Provence this beautiful bright day in the summer of 2002. While Joe parked the car, I walked around the port and was attracted to a little Kiosk advertising "Calanques." The sign read, "8 Calanques—15 Euros, 6 Calanques—12 Euros, 3 Calanques-8 Euros." The sign made it appear as though we would be buying those Calanques, not just viewing them. Nevertheless, by the time Joe returned from parking our car, I smilingly held up two Calanques tickets for us to see the eight Calanques.

In a few minutes we boarded a very classy yacht and the tour guide began his description of what we were about to see. I suddenly realized that the tour guide would be speaking only French, meaning I would not understand a word. But what we did see were magnificent geological formations like few places on earth. As we left the harbor and turned west, we saw the first of the eight Calanques. They were beautiful white, almost marble-like, cliffs with all kinds of rugged sharp edges and shapes. The first one was called Port Miou and it was several hundred feet high. We sailed down a channel large enough to accommodate 600 yachts. At the end of it was a white sandy beach where hundreds of people were swimming. Our boat sailed to the rocky edge of the beach and then turned around and headed out to the Mediterranean and toward the next inlet.

We took a right turn as we reached the Mediterranean and motored a quarter mile or so to the second Calanque. Our vessel bobbed up and down along the rocky shores and in about fifteen minutes we were at the Calanque. We motored inland into the next Calanque that was not as deep as the first but its limestone carvings were even more beautiful.

During the next three hours we would sail into each of the eight Calanques, which were from a quarter mile to a mile long. Each one was different from its neighbor but yet very picturesque with steep rocky limestone formation on either side. Limestone is a rather soft rock so the wind and the water carved many designs and much imagery into their rocky surfaces. One had a deep hole into the face of the rock. Another had a gash several hundred feet high into its side. Most of the limestone surfaces had no vegetation but every once in awhile we would see an individual tree or shrub standing majestically alone on the top or the side of a cliff. The green of the shrub stood out in deep contrast to the white of the cliffs magnificent sides. I can recall one tree, not very tall, but standing by itself on the top of a cliff, I wondered how in the world it ever got there and I thought it must have been so lonely. Our vessel went from inlet to inlet each more beautiful than its neighbor.

The last and most spectacular of the Calanques is called En Vau (meaning the view in French). Its white cliffs and jagged edges along the entire mile-long length are just magnificent. At the end of the narrow inlet was a pure white sandy beach where sunbathers and swimmers were spending a calm and peaceful day. Our boat slowly maneuvered its way to the end of the Calanques. Our captain carefully made his way between dozens of other boats to the very end of the deep inlet and pulled up to an outcropping of rocks. From the bow (front) of our vessel about ten passengers with knapsacks and lunch boxes disembarked onto these rocky shores. They climbed upon the rocks, making their way to the beach. They would spend the day at shore and take a subsequent boat back to Cassis.

Now our boat carefully reversed its course, and retraced its way back to the open Mediterranean Sea. On the way back to the port at Cassis our vessel went somewhat further out into the Med so we were able to get a different view of the wonderful contrast between the blue Mediterranean and the chalk white cliffs of the Calanques. It was a wonderful trip down the length of the Calanques to En Vau and an equally beautiful trip back to Cassis.

On shore Joe and I found a little restaurant just one street off the port street. It was called Napoleon Bonaparte and had some great French food. After lunch we reluctantly bid farewell to this very interesting little town and its chalk white cliffs. Joe and I now have added the word, Calanques to our travel vocabulary.

Village of Cassis, on the Mediterranean Sea, Southern France,

2. First Address in Western Europe

A few weeks before I left for Marseilles, I told a friend that I was going to travel to southern France. He said "Oh! You mean to the Riviera." I let him know that there is a lot more to southern France than the Rivera. It was only after my trip that I realized how true my statement was. In the sixteen days traveling all over the south of France, Joe and I did not see a single millionaire's villa or a multimillion-dollar yacht or even a movie star. What we did see were unusually historic sites like the Temple in the center of the modern city Nimes and the Arles coliseum where gladiators fought for their lives two millennia ago.

The history of this part of France is significant because it was the passageway of the Greeks, and later the Romans from Italy to Spain, as far back as 26 centuries ago. So many towns around southern France have an historic tie to the ancient Greeks and Romans but the town, which most impressed me from an historic point of view was a place called Glanum.

For almost 1800 years, from the third to the twentieth century, this little place, about 100 acres in area between two cliffs, was buried in dust and dirt. Until 1925 only two structures peered above the ground level. They were the top of a tower and a mausoleum. Everyone in the area knew they must have been very old but no one ever did much about it.

About two miles away however, a city called St. Remy dated back to the Middle Ages. It grew up, and had its own history by virtue of a brilliant scientist, Nostradamus who lived there in the seventeenth century. He became famous for his writings about the future of the world. Another reason for St. Remy's fame was Vincent Van Gogh, the famous artist. He spent his last years there, a mentally ill patient in the local hospital. Vincent loved walking the fields of St. Remy, painting the trees, houses, and sunflowers but never realizing that under his feet existed such history.

Forty years after Van Gogh's tragic death, a pair of archeologists walked down the road from St. Remy and looked quizzically at the two old structures and said, "there must be more here than meets the eye." First they dug near the surface and close to the mausoleum, then they began to dig deeper and in the direction of the two cliffs a few hundred yards away. At last, they found a "treasure chest"—an ancient city. It took almost thirty years until the middle of the 1970s to scope out the extent of the city that the history books called, Glanum after a god that the ancient people worshiped known as Glan.

The city was first founded by the Greeks about 2600 hundred years ago, when the people traveling in that area found water near the edge of narrow corridor between the two cliffs. The cliffs gave them protection and the water gave them sustenance, so Glanum was developed.

As Joe and I walked the ancient streets of Glanum one warm sunny June day, it was exciting to see the results of the archeologists and how they put together the big pieces of limestone in order to resurrect the city . To me it looked like a huge three-dimensional jigsaw puzzle. They found the pieces that went into the temples, houses, swimming pools and forums surrounding an open market. In addition to a water storage system, the archeologists also found a sewage system under the main street leading to a deep waste area. One factor they discovered was that the Greeks buried their dead outside of the walls of the city. Hence, the mausoleum was far from the center of the city. It must have taken a great deal of imagination to figure out which stones went into which house.

As we walked down the street there were stones lying all over the place attesting to the difficulty of the task. One of the stones had the name Agrippa from the Roman times carved upon it. Historians believe that Agrippa was the name of Augusta, Caesar's son-in-law. So, it is possible that he spent his summers in southern France (Gaul). I like to think of his address as the first in Western Europe.

The city probably existed for over eight hundred years, first Grecian, then Roman and then mysteriously disappearing prior to the dark ages. Archeologists believe that undisturbed areas seemed to get covered with dust and dirt at the rate of about one foot every hundred years so that Glanum was about 16 to 18 feet deep when the excavation work was done. It must have taken an incredible amount of digging even to find the exact place.

I have walked the ancient streets near the center of Athens (like the Agora and the Parthenon), the streets of Pompeii in Italy and the two millinnium old city of Ephasis in Turkey. Now I can add southern France and the city of Glanum to the list of places where the Greeks and Romans took up residence.

Joe Burros at ancient ruins of Glanum. France.

Ancient Roman Temple in the midst of a modern city—Nimes, France

3. The ABC's of Southern France

Southern France has a history rich with so many towns built in the last two thousand years. We visited a variety of places during our two weeks stay and each of them is part of the pattern of this country 's very impressive past. Our trip became a history lesson of one sort or another. Traveling throughout the land was an exciting way of learning French history. I am now calling it the ABC's of southern France.

A. Arenas and Aqueducts.

In the earliest days of European history the Romans were great builders .Two thousand years ago the Romans brought from the center of their civilization the concept of entertainment of the masses. Amazingly the two huge structures which they built in southern France similar to the coliseum in Rome still exist, These two arenas in Arles and Nimes are almost identical to each other and must have been constructed by the same group of craftsmen. Of all the structures that we saw in southern France, the arenas and aqueducts gave me the most vivid feeling of the abilities of their engineering prowess. They also give the traveler a good feeling of what life must have been like twenty centuries ago.

When Joe and I walked the length and breath of the arena in Nimes, we felt as though we were living in 100 A. D., arriving in the arena to watch gladiators struggle with each other for life or death. Because it was a very brutal time the Romans accepted the death of man or beast very casually. In Nimes we learned that the development of Christianity was to a certain extent the result of the objection to this cruelty. Those arenas were the center of entertainment for the masses in those days. Tremendously large audiences of as many as 20,000 Roman citizens would jam the arenas to watch the brutality of the times. One interesting fact we learned was that each class of citizen had his own entrance and seating section. When they arrived on the day of combat, every citizen knew what entrance to use and where they would sit so they did not mix with the people of other classes.

Surprisingly, both arenas have existed for two thousand years and the arena in Nimes is still used for concerts. (The arena in Arles is in much worse condition and is treated as a historical monument). In our country those structures would have never lasted as long because we would have destroyed them long ago in the name of progress. As a comparison when I was in my twenties, New York had an arena known as Madison Square Garden. We have taken down two such arenas with that same name during my lifetime. We seem to have no such loyalty to our history, whereas the Europeans treat their structures with great reverence.

Another very important type of structure which was built in the days of the Roman Empire was the very functional aqueduct. In the early days of community living in Europe the towns developed around their water wells. Almost every city in Germany, France and England can trace their origins to the Romans and their respect for the water supply. The population of the city of Marseilles however out-stripped their local water supply so the Romans realized they had to bring water in from the outlaying areas. Long before they knew of the concept of gravity they instinctively knew water would not flow uphill so they built canals that would allow the water to flow down from the hills to Marseilles. But they had to cross low laying areas and thus they developed the concept of aqueducts. The one huge structure which still stands after eighteen centuries is the Pont de Duct. It is over 80 meters high and contains two levels of bridges that extend over one thousand meters in length. The concept was still used eighteen centuries later, when a new aqueduct was built in the 1880's outside of Aix en Provence to increase its water supply.

The aqueduct we visited was built in the late 1880's. and was tremendously impressive. It had three separate arched sections, each one hundreds of feet high and each one built upon the other. It was so large both in height and length that

I could not take a picture of the entire unit. But by using a video camera, we were able to get an impression of its size. So A in my history lesson is for arenas and aqueducts.

Aqueduct outside of Aix en Provence. Southern France

B. Bridges

In the alphabet of early history the B stands for bridges. The entire area of southern France is crisscrossed with beautiful rivers necessitating many historic bridges. They were built to meet the transportation needs of the traveler. The earliest and most historic is the bridge across the Rhone called the Pont St. Benezet. The story goes that it was started in the year 1150. Apparently, the pope, not wanting to have the bridge built set up a contest that was an almost impossible task, read that anyone who could pick up one huge stone chosen by a religious order would have the right to take charge of the building of a bridge across the Rhone River. The were sure no one could thereby the river would never be bridged. But to their surprise, a shepard boy, named Benezet, magically was able pick up and actually throw the stone. He managed the construction of the bridge which had 22 individual spans and because of his feat was honored with sainthood. About four centuries later, in the year 1550 a terrible storm destroyed all but four of the spans. Now those four spans and a small chapel still go out about half way into the Grande Rhone River and, tourists for the sum of 3 Euros(about $3.50), can walk out into the Rhone on this 800 year old span. Joe and I walked out and back to the middle of the Rhone River by means of the old bridge.

Joe and I spent one day traveling from the city of Nimes to Rodez following the River Tarn (Tarn du Garn). The Tarn is a rapidly moving river with steep magnificent rugged cliffs on either side. The single lane road parallels the river and every few miles there is a little town cut into the hillside. The driving was tedious because of the narrow lanes and hair pin turns which makes for a slow trip. In the middle of the day we stopped at the village, La Merene and I walked across the narrow single lane bridge while Joe rested. The Tarn was about fifty feet below the town and at the river's edge was a clear sandy beach and tourists rented canoes or kyacks and paddled down the next ten miles of rather mildly rocky streams. They were then taken in vans upstream to their cars. The bridge across the river Tarn at La Merene was one of the only modern bridges in the area. The town was a sixteenth century village with stone houses and one or two narrow winding streets built right into the mountain. Every town we stopped at this day was a scenic beauty.

After walking the length of La Merene and its bridge, I came back to the car to find Joe up and ready to drive once more. We stopped off many times during that day's journey—at overlooks in the mountains, at little towns and hamlets along the river, and at wayside chapels. I could have spent a week along the Tarn, not merely one day.

After spending the week with our friends, Robert and Carol's house, in Salacroup, we were ready to conclude our trip with the final two days in Toulouse.
Carol told us to be sure to stop on the way at the city of Cahors and see the
bridge called Pont Valentry. She told us it is a very beautiful bridge and worth
seeing.

When we reached Cahors, we decided to stop for lunch by the river's edge and
see the bridge. We fortunately found a parking place near the river and went into
a small restaurant adjacent to the river. From our outdoor table we had a perfect
view of the bridge It had three high towers, one at each end and one in the middle—each different from the other. I took some beautiful pictures of them and
then we were off again to Toulouse and our final leg of our journey.

Toulouse was the biggest city we saw in the last two weeks with about one-half
million people. The old city, that was at one time part of Spain and at another
time independent, has a very different feel from the rest of Southern France. The
people of Toulouse look darker skinned and more like Algerians. The streets are
very narrow and are rather dingy with lots of graffiti all over.

Because of the density of the buildings and people on the streets, it took us
quite a while to find our hotel which turned out to be right in the center of town.
It was just across the street from the old imperial palace, Now the palace is used
as a concert hall. We were staying only one day so that early the next morning we
went to the river to see the city from the river side. We arranged to take a boat
ride in the afternoon. The city is inland on the Garonne River but because of an
arrangement of canals one can actually go from the Atlantic Ocean near the port
of Bordeaux to the Mediterranean Sea by means of a series of canal locks.

One bridge across the Garonne that was built in the twelfth century had a very
interesting history. One end was built in solid stone and was rigid but the other
end was constructed in earth. Shortly after its construction, the end built in mud,
slipped down about ten feet before to many years went by. It finally reached bed-
rock and became stable. Now as you take a boat trip down the Garonne, the
bridge looks quite unbalanced, but we are told it is nevertheless quite safe.

Partially Destroyed Bridge Over Grande Rhone River, Avignon, France,

C. Chateaus, Churches and Cathedrals

The "C" of the ABC's stands for cathedrals, chateaus and caves. There are scores of cathedrals but one of the most impressive is the one in Marseilles that stands on the highest point in the city. There is so much to see in Marseilles, we could barely scratch the surface. We took a little bus around the city. We started our trip from the steps of the cathedral at the top of the hill and wound our way down to little streets and eventually ended at the waterfront.

The entire area of southern France has scores of interesting historical chateaus. Joe and I stopped off at a bookstore in St. Cere with Carol and Katie one day. I glanced at a book about chateaus of France and I was shocked when I realized just how many Chateaus there are. There must be hundreds dating back to the tenth century.

We visited at least one half dozen chateaus—from the Les Beau, built in the tenth century to Collenge Rouge (named after the red sandstone found in the local area)—to Rockamadour an incredibly beautiful Chateau and its entire town built into the side of a cliff to Montel built just outside of St. Cere—to the Ventbret, outside of Aix en Provence almost entirely destroyed over the past five hundred years.

One of the most interesting chateaus to me was the one called Montel. It was a family castle for almost four hundred years, but in the late nineteenth century it was bought by a man whose goal was to make money selling off its contents. He sold off dozens of artifacts of the Chateau to private individuals and museums all around the world.

Then in the early twentieth century a philanthropist bought the Montel Chateau and recognized how it had been violated and how wonderful it would be if only it could be brought back to its original condition. He then went around the world tracing the location of every one of the Chateau's missing furniture, carpeting, tapestry, art work and statuary. With a few exceptions that are statues in museums in New York and Philadelphia he repurchased every item sold off by the previous owner. It has now been reassembled to its original sixteenth century condition with the exception of a few statues that had to be copied from the original. I saw this as a wonderful example of philanthropy winning over greed.

Joe and I spent hours touring the Chateau and viewing its beautiful contents. It was especially interesting to see since we knew of the effort that was taken to restore this landmark.

4. Les Beau Dynasty

Sixty years ago when I was a student at Brooklyn Tech I took a course which was one of the special subjects that distinguished Tech from the other schools in the New York City. The course was Industrial Processes (affectionately known as IP). In it, we were taught all about the manufacturing of different materials. It explained how the materials used in the manufacturing processes were made. For example, we were told how glass, paper, steel and aluminum were made from the raw materials, right up to the finished product. Until I took that course, I had never heard the word bauxite before. During the course I was taught that the light-weight but very tough metal, aluminum, was processed from an ore found in the ground called bauxite. Although the course was very comprehensive, the instructor never told us where the word bauxite came from. Mind you, not knowing that fact did not severely hinder my ability to succeed during the next sixty years. The fact is that I never gave a thought about bauxite or its origins.

By now you may be asking what does all this have to do with my trip to southern France. You are about to find out.

There we were in southern France and told we were about to visit a magnificent ancient town built in the cliffs by a very wealthy and powerful family in the fifteenth century named Les Beau (pronounced la bow). The family was extremely rich and powerful and constructed a huge chateau which could have almost been considered a fortress, The huge Le Beau chateau rested almost one quarter of a mile along the top of the cliff and down below, the Les Beau family built the village where all the supporting staff, resided.

Their name, Les Beau, had nothing to do with aluminum until the nineteenth century when two metallurgists discovered that the ore found in the mountains of Les Beau could be processed and formed into the metal, aluminum. They needed to have a name for the ore being mined and processed. Since it was being taken from the mines in and around Les Beau, they decided to call it bauxite. Nowadays even though the ore comes from other parts of the world, mostly Africa, the miners still call it bauxite,

Joe and I drove in, parked at one end of Les Beau and walked along the old town street whose little stone homes were now souvenir shops, restaurants, ice parlor, and bed and breakfast inns. When we reached the end there was a small museum showing the history of the chateau, and then for six Euros we received an audio guide and permission to visit the entire area. The recording was in English and gave us a complete history of the Chateau and the Les Beau dynasty, who lived there for about ten generations. The audio guide made the trip through the Les Beau much more understandable. We walked the entire length of the area. I took many minutes of video and Joe took lots of still photos. We spent several hours there and enjoyed every minute of it. From the height of the Chateau cliffs there were incredible views of the surrounding countryside.

One of the most impressive aspects of Southern France are the medieval chateaus. The one at Les Beau is by far the most interesting. One section of the chateau I found most fascinating was the pigeon and chicken coops. Built into the limestone cliffs at one end of the Chateau, the coops consisted of hundreds of little cubicles where the pigeons and chickens would lay their eggs, a major source of food for the people of the sixteenth century. They also built a very advanced water storage system that provided water throughout the Les Beau village. Another impressive sight is family chapel that remains in good shape after five centuries.

When we completed the tour we stopped at a little snack shop to get a much-needed drink. To our surprise we heard English being spoken at the next table. We struck up a conversation with a couple from Southern California on their honeymoon, and before we knew it we were exchanging travel experiences.

They told us about a place called the Cathedral of Images which was just two miles away. Our newly acquainted friends, however, said, "We don't want to tell you about it, because we want it to be a surprise." The man said, "Just trust us. You will find it, a truly remarkable experience."

Chicken and Pigeon Coops, Les Beau, France

5. The Cathedral Of Images

For well over one half a century the hills and valleys of Les Beau were busy places with an industrial beehive of activity. Truck after truck would leave the mines of this once sleepy little town with its valuable cargo of ore. This once sleepy little farming area was turned into a very different sort of place. Suddenly, the hills of southern France became alive with a valuable mineral called Bauxite. This ore was converted into a lighter weight material, aluminum, used in the manufacture of aircraft.

Ton after ton of this ore came rolling out of the hills of southern France and into the factories of Toulouse and other processing plants around the country. But gradually economics overtook the business and it became cheaper to process the ore in other parts of the world where the cost of labor and power was so much less and this once-sleepy little area of southern France found it self asleep again with nothing to do but raise goats for cheese and grapes for wine.

Soon, though, a new valued opportunity, roared on to the world's market. It became the age of tourism. All over the world, cities and towns were trying to cash in on this very valuable business. From the seaports of Boston and Baltimore to the old fortresses of Louisburg in Newfoundland, Canada to the harbor of Marseille, history was becoming an intregal part of tourism.

The ancient towns of southern France were no different. The cities of Arles and Avignon had wonderfully historical sites to attract new post World War II tourists. Suddenly everywhere Vincent, Pablo, Claude or Toulouse, slept became a tourist attraction. Interestingly, it was the development of the large (jumbo) jet aircraft (made possible by the discovery of bauxite and resultant metal, aluminum, that made large scale economic travel possible. Entrepreneurs in Southern France continued looking to find ways of attracting more of these tourists. Every little town and hamlet were soon looking into its reservoir of assets to find ways to cash in on this multibillion dollar tourist market. The town of Les Beau was not different. They looked into their treasure chest of assets and, of course, the first very valuable asset was the ancient town of the Les Beau itself. A wonderful tourist attraction, with its one thousand year old Chateau perched high up on its scenic cliff, would certainly became a five star attraction. But the question soon arose what else in the area could keep the tourist a while longer. It certainly was not the goats grazing in the fields and there were no wineries like those of Bordeaux or Napa Valley .

Then, a pair of ingenuous young men looked to the huge hole sitting at the bottom of a large mountain where for fifty years the bauxite was taken out of the earth. Just what could possibly be done with a hole about 100 feet high and the size of three or four football fields. Then in the late nineteen nineties they came up with a wonderful idea. Why not turn this huge cavern into an audio and visual extravaganza. But it would have to be something unique and attractive enough to interest the average tourist. They originated what these two men called, the Cathedral of Images.

Joe and I saw the result of their five years of labor in 2003. If you remember from the previous story entitled, Les Beau Dynasty, we met two a couple from Southern California who recommended we visit the Cathedral Of Images but they would not tell us what it was—this was the surprise.

As we bought tickets at six Euros each, the cashier gave us a woolen blanket to wrap around our shoulders. She told us that the temperature in the mine remains 55 degrees Fahrenheit all year long. As we entered, there was a description about the idea and its result. The entrepreneurs used the concept of an artist's exhibition from the 16th century named Pieter Bruegal who painted people and scenes from all over Holland. His works are in museums all over the world.

As we walked in I could not see anything, but Joe said "Those pictures are great". But I still saw nothing. My transition eye glasses were still in full sunglass mode. I realized it takes a while for them to change back to normal clear glass. During that time I could not see much at all. After a while I began to see the huge pictures flashing all over the walls of the caves. The pictures, copies of paintings by the famous artist Pieter Bruegal, were synchronized with wonderful classical music presentations by Mozart and Mussorsky. The Mussorsky pieces, I recall, were Night On Bald Mountain and Pictures At An Exhibition. The names of those pieces were absolutely appropriate to the art program in the hollowed—out mine. The Bruegel art and the music presentation was spectacularly coordinated with tremendous fidelity.

Joe later wrote me, "I enjoyed the selections very much. It seemed to suit the art work. My impression of the cathedral was like going into another reality. The longer I stayed in there the more I settled into this other world. It was nice to spend some time and look at the details of the painting. Seeing the show made me want to see more of the artwork of Bruegel."

My conclusion was the video show was especially interesting in that they showed Pieter Bruegal's pictures from so many aspects. The art coordinators isolated small sections of paintings and then blew them up in some cases as much as one hundred times. For example a small boy's face in an original painting was now a twenty by thirty feet picture with incredible detail. There must have been five or six gigantic rooms deep under ground each with a Bruegal painting flashing at you from all over. We walked from room to room listening to the music of Mozart and Mossorsky while viewing Bruegel 's magnificent art. I stayed about thirty minutes but gradually the cold seeped under my blanket and I left about one half hour before Joe.

I would have enjoyed it more if they had chairs to rest in between presentation galleries and to use while listening and seeing the program. In any case, I give the developers a lot of credit for coming up with an idea to take an old mine and make it into a money maker. Only time will tell whether or not it will continue to be successful.

6. Department 46—A Secret Hideaway

France has 96 Departments. A French travel editor on French National Radio who is also a memory expert was asked to name all the departments in France from 1 to 96. He started from 1 and went up the line. When he got to 46 he said that he would not name that department because it is such a wonderful place he did not want anybody to know about it. So he skipped 46 and went down the line naming all the rest.

But my readers, you are going to be lucky and I am going to spill the beans and tell you where and all about department 46.

It is called the Lot and it is in the south of France, and truly a wonderful place to visit. If you Americans are concerned about the reception you may get while visiting in Department 46 you need not worry. They hardly know America exists. The Lot has no big cities but scores of tiny towns, hamlets, and neighborhoods. My map of The Lot listed 350 towns and villages and probably dozens more not even listed.

The nearest medium size town to where Robert and Carol, Joe's friends, live is St. Cere. I especially liked this town with its center square and streets of well kept houses. Down the center of town are a quiet little stream and pretty little park with the Chateau being only a few kilometers from there.

The next smallest town is a place called Gorses. It has about fifty or so homes, an inn, a restaurant, a gas station, store, and a post office The man in the store was very helpful to Joe when we first arrived in the area. Joe had been to Salacroup several times before, but the roads are so small and winding that he could not find the little turnoff to Salacroup. We stopped in Gorses and this very helpful man in the store told us the easy way to Salacroup.

Salacroup is very small. It has one road, about ten houses and probably thirty or so people, and an equal number of dogs and chickens. It amazes me how somebody can even find a place as small. Salacroup is not even on the map of the Lot.

Robert and Carol found out about the Lot in 1995 when a friend in California told them about the place. Robert first went over by himself and then both of them explored the place until they finally found their dream house in Salacroup. It is an old stone house that needed the likes of a Robert Cabrera to turn it into a quaint comfortable home. Robert's love is homework. Not the kind you get at school but fixing up an old homestead with tender loving care. That is the kind of homework he loves. If someone would ask Robert what his hobby is he would say home repair. If someone would ask him what his profession is he would probably say home repair. If someone would ask him what he does in his spare time, he would say home repair. The house they found in 1996 was the perfect place for Robert.

He has spent these last seven or eight years fixing up the place to his heart's delight. He expanded the kitchen, turned three small rooms into one great room that is now so inviting and comfortable. The thing I loved best was the big old fireplace. One rainy day after walking the length of Salacroup I came in chilled to the bone. Carol, noticing my discomfort, built a fire in the huge fireplace and in a few minutes the room was warm and toasty. With the fire and a few blankets that Carol thoughtfully placed around me, I was feeling fine in no time.

Over the years Robert worked on dozens of other projects large and small. Robert's frustration with working in France is getting the tools and equipment that he needs to buy for his projects. For example, he showed me a power table saw and said that he had to bring this from Berkeley, California because the French-made equivalent "just falls apart in a year or so" (or less). As we went around the house he showed me all the things that he carried almost half around the world rather than buy a French equivalent. I was really surprised at this, because all the things that he brought from the USA were in almost every case made in the orient (Japan, China, etc.). I had always thought that a French company could build items as good as they could in the Far East. Apparently that is not the case. Robert has spent many years upgrading and refurbishing homes in the Berkeley, California area, so he knows what he is talking about.

As we went through the house he told me some of his future plans, like a recreation room and a new entrance through it to the main house. But shortly after he bought this house in Salacroup he found another house across the street that needs even more work than the current house. But that does not faze him in the slightest. It just means that he has more exciting projects to do in the next few years.

A few days after I arrived I began to hear the word Pressoir ("oir" pronounced as a "w.") Robert would say "I am going to the Pressoir" or "the Pressoir will get a new roof" or "the Pressoir needs something." I did not want to show my ignorance so I did not ask about the Pressoir. Then I found out a day or two later when Robert asked if I would like to go to see the Pressoir. Well, the Pressoir is not exactly a town or a hamlet. It is a group of buildings with a street sign announcing its location, and also the name of Robert's latest project. Robert and I drove about six kilometers over one of the most beautiful country roads, up hills and down into valleys and around sharp bends. At last through a tiny hamlet, on the right side of the road was a sign with the single word 'Pressoir'. One hundred yards or so later Robert turned off the road into a dirt trail. In front of us was a stone barn, and to the left was a pretty run-down stone house and on the right was yet another barn. Robert turned off the engine and announced, "This is the Pressoir." One would have to say that the Pressoir is probably the smallest hamlet in France since its population would have to be listed as "0" because even Robert doesn't live there, he just owns it. However, at one time or other in its history the Pressoir did have several families so it would have had some population.

Robert cut the grass in the field outside of the stone house, while I walked around this very little "hamlet." The view from the front of the property is just spectacular. The land sloped down across the road and one can see a half dozen farms in every direction often separated by rows of tall thin poplars. The air was so clear I could see for miles to the hills lining the horizon. The farm on the opposite side of the road had a herd of diary cows grazing in the afternoon's sun. As I stood there, the cows drifted in from an adjacent field and soon were sitting in front of their watering hole right across the road from the Pressoir, jealously guarding it against trespassers like Robert or me. They made it clear that we would not be allowed to take even a sip of water. That herd of cows was the only unfriendly souls I ever saw in France that year.

After Robert did his chores he showed me around the house. He indicated where he would install an indoor bathroom, where he would enlarge the bedroom and add a kitchen. When Robert talks about his projects his face lights up and you can see how he envisions the work. But for now Robert's immediate project is to put a roof on the barn so that it does not collapse. Before we left, Robert decided to show me the rest of the Pressoir that consisted of a broken down shed, a pigsty and the soon-to-be obsolescent outhouse. Our day trip to Pressoir was quite an experience. I would call it a town in need of work.

Joe and I stayed for seven wonderful days in The Lot. We saw caves with 20,000 years old artwork, villages picturesquely built in the 16th century on the side of cliffs and bridges of unique beauty, but these will be the subjects of other stories. For now I was content to spend some peaceful time walking among the little villages of the Lot where the troubles of Iraq, Liberia and North Korea seemed very far away.

7. The Caves of Pech Merle

After spending a week with Robert and Carol in their two hundred year old stone house in Salacroup, Joe and I were read to complete our trip by visiting Toulouse and then flying back to the USA. The night before we were to leave, Carol said, "Are you going to stop off at Pech Merle?"

"What's Pech Merle?" I asked.

"They are some of the most spectacular caves in Southern France. You must stop off and see them."

With that Carol jumps up and goes for the phone. In a minute she returns, all smiles, "You are lucky. We were able to get you in for the eleven o'clock tour."

Then she explained, "It is so popular. They take only fifty people an hour. It's set up for tomorrow and remember to dress warmly."

The next morning Joe and I left at nine sharp. We drove on the highway for over an hour and soon found ourselves going up higher and higher into the hilliest section of southwestern France. The road became narrow and very winding. We were soon going back and forth around a series of sharp switchbacks. It was almost eleven and I began to think that we would be late for our reservation. Then all of a sudden, we reached the end of the road and saw the sign—Caves of Pech Merle. At last we had arrived. It was not a moment too soon. Remembering what Carol said about putting on our sweaters, we grabbed our jackets and headed for the entrance.

In a deep French accent the receptionist, looks at us skeptically and asks, "Do you gentlemen have reservations?" To which we answer, trying to sound French "Oh, of course Madame,"

"The tour is about to begin," she said in an impatient tone of voice. "The group is gathering inside."

She pointed in the direction of a small conference room. There must have been fifty people already listening to the guide who, of course, was speaking French. With Joe's help I was able to get the gist of the history of this place that is as follows:

One day in early 1922 two teenage French boys who lived in the area were busily playing in the hills as fifteen year olds do. They had been playing there for years but on this day they found an opening which lead down to a path they had never seen before. This path seemed to go further and deeper than any they had explored. They decided to follow it and to determine if there was another way out.

But it did not go out. It went deeper and deeper. Although it was quite dark, they suddenly saw markings on a cave wall that was fortunately caught by a ray of light. There appeared to be pictures or markings of some kind. The next day they asked a preacher-friend to come with them and see if he would know what the writing or markings were. So, as the story goes, the rest is history.

The more people who went down, the more excited the new findings were becoming. Soon archeologists from Paris arrived and found that the writings were indeed ancient hieroglyphics. When they brought bigger lights into the cave, they discovered the pictures were of horses, bison, wooly mammoths and the like.

With that story as the beginning of our tour, we started our trip down into those million year old magnificent caves. As soon as we started to descend, we knew the reason for wearing sweaters. It was both cold and damp as the temperature remained at about 55 degrees Fahrenheit throughout the year. Without our jackets, we most assuredly would have been very uncomfortable.

We walked slowly and carefully down a long narrow lane. After about ten minutes, we arrived at a huge theater-like circular cavernous arena two hundred feet in diameter. There on the opposite side of the room was the most dramatic of wall paintings I had ever seen. Bathed in mellow lights that enhanced its beauty and impressive size, we stood in awe.

Ten years before I read an article in National Geographic describing these caves and in particular the wall painting of those horses, but until I saw them in person, I could not imagine how impressive they were. To think that prehistoric man could have painted these pictures before the advent of paints, brushes and canvas! I was extremely impressed with the perfect perspective and depth perception these painting showed from all around the huge room.

Of course we could not understand the French guide but later he came to us and spoke in English about the paintings. Although the horses were probably painted using a form of charcoal taken from the remains of old fires, the handprints were stenciled on the wall. The guide told us that the Cro-Magnon man who did them probably put a colored berry juice in his mouth and blew the liquefied matter toward his hand resting upon the wall. This caused a stencil-like drawing perfectly outlining his five fingers and palm. There are six such stenciled drawings around the pair of horses, three along the top and three along the bottom. The guide explained that these handprints were in fact the signature of the artist. He probably placed six of them around the painting in the event some wore off with time. The most miraculous part of the scene however is they have lasted these scores of centuries despite the moisture, dripping water, and aging of these works of art.

We walked for about one hour through the long series of caves that even without the hieroglyphics were very spectacular. There were huge rooms, some more than 50 feet high with stalactites and stalagmites formed from the slowly dripping waters seeping through the limestone ceilings. The colors and the shapes are so spectacular that one can imagine even the Cro-Magnon people would have been impressed. The caves may have been there for millions of years so they probably looked very similar even 18,000 years ago. A few feet from one of the hieroglyphic pictures was a footprint made as a result of a prehistoric man stepping into mud. One of the ancient people probably stepped into wet dirt and left a print. It must have dried and hardened over these many thousands of years.

Even though the walking at times was difficult because of the steep and narrow lanes, it was an exciting and unforgettable few hours. I now understood why Carol did not want us to miss Pech Merle. She was right. It was a historic experience never to be forgotten.

As we left, I wondered why, of all those people who traveled from Rome to Spain during the last two thousand years, none of them stumbled into these caves. All those who built the cities of Aries, Avignon and Nimes, those who constructed the arenas and aqueducts, all those developers of the chateaus and cathedrals for hundreds of years, those travelers who covered the length and breath of southern Europe—all of these never discovered these ancient caves. It amazingly was two teenagers in the early twentieth century who stumbled upon this priceless ancient archeological find.

It made me realize that there may still be many more things on earth yet to discover.

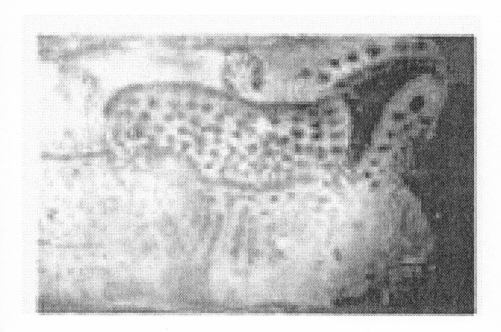

Ancient Cave Art, Pech Merle, Southern France,

8. The Room At Monet's Place

On our 2004 trip to France, Lila and I decided to visit Giverny, the town where the famous painter, Claude Monet, spent the last half of his eighty six years.

During those years, Monet was often in a controversy with the local citizens to keep industry and commerce out. After all, Monet did not want the place where he had developed such beautiful ponds, flower gardens and Japanese bridges to be spoiled by the introduction of a factory to build bricks and mortar. He and some of the other citizens of Giverny did not want their picturesque little town to be spoiled by the introduction of the places that would show the signs of capitalism as opposed to art and culture.

"No" said Claude Monet the epitome of impressionistic art of the late nineteenth century. With his influence he kept out of Giverny that dreaded factory and their town stayed the way Monet wanted it to be.

During his later years, wealth and fame followed him without his even trying to get it. People from all over the world came to Giverny to see those beautiful lily ponds and Japanese bridges that were the subject of so many of his paintings.

But alas business and capitalism follows art whether the artist likes it or not. The tourists who came by the thousands to see his works also needed to go to rest rooms and wanted a glass of wine or water, and before long his friends and business manager convinced him that he needed to build a structure to supply those facilities. It was going to cost a significant amount of money to build such a building. They then figured that while building such a structure it might as well have the capability to sell copies of Monet's works of art. Now the twentieth century caught up to the artist who wanted to keep Giverny so pure and idylic. The conflict of beauty and business came to a head as Monet now pushed to have a two-story gift shop erected on one corner of his three-acre property. His fellow countrymen had to remind Claude how he had advocated not building a factory twenty years before.

So art sucombed to commerce and business. The man who fought so hard to keep the factory out of Giverny now advocated for the construction of a 1,000 square-meter gift shop.

Alas, I sat in the gift shop on this rainy autumn day waiting to use the rest room and thinking how grateful I was that Monet had won in the battle to give us fans the place we needed.

Bridge at Monet's Place, Giverny, France,

9. Paris: The City of Beauty

Lila and I spent our first four days in Europe the fall of 2004, in my most favorite city, Paris. It is uniquely pretty situated on the very scenic river Seine. One of the reasons for its beautiful image, Is that the winding river just wraps itself around the city in a most interesting way. Everything looks best from the excursion boats, which wander up and down the river. On one end of the trip you suddenly come face to face with what appears to be the Statue of Liberty—of course it is just a miniature copy. But when one thinks of the statue in our New York harbor, made by donations of French francs from French children, and by the labor of French workmen, you cannot but feel they are entitled to the first trial piece.

Before leaving, I began studying about the upcoming trip. I had not been in Paris for a decade, so a refresher course seemed appropriate. One night about a week before we would be leaving for Paris I asked Joe, my cousin and traveling companion, for the most important sights we should visit, other than the usual ones.

Of course Lila and I would be going to the Louvre Museum because we were staying at the Hotel due Louvre right across the Rue Ravioli. Joe gave me several other places that he felt were also important. Because he had spent many summers in Paris while he was learning French, I felt his opinions would have a lot of merit.

The first place he mentioned was the Carnetvalet Museum—it is the museum of the city of Paris. Then he suggested that while we were in that part of Paris to first stop at the Parc Visages, one of the oldest parks in modern civilization. It is rather small but with very formally cut trees in foursquare corners. In the center is a statue of Louis XII on a horse. After viewing the park, he suggested we go to Carnetvalet, a museum comparable to Versailles. It was a spectacular place.

The one place I did not see was Versailles. I had planned on visiting it but there were too many other things on our schedule. I thought seeing the rooms in Carnetvalet was a fair substitute.

Then, because he had parks on his mind, Joe suggested Parc Monceau. He mentioned several other places. But, by this time I was on overload and would be swamped if I just went to these places.

Of course, we did see the Louvre, Lila went one afternoon and saw many of the classical paintings. One of her favorites, The Raft of Medusa was unfortunately not on exhibition. I went the next day and saw the entire room of magnificent marble sculptures. It was one of the most magnificent of displays. I also saw the most famous of sculptures, called Winged Victory.

Then, one evening after dinner we took a slow walk from our hotel to the Louvre courtyard where I. M. Pei placed his very controversial Pyramids. We each had our new digital cameras and we played around with them like kids with new Christmas toys.

Our visit reinforced my opinion that Paris is the most beautiful city on earth.

Louvre Museum at midnight, Paris

Seine River through Paris

Parc Monceau, with its 16th Century columns, Paris'

10. The Oktoberfest

Four General Instrument marketers exhibiting at the electronic show in the 1980s left Weisbaden for a day of relaxation. We arrived by train in Munich shortly before noon of October first—the beginning of Oktoberfest. The crowds were coming in from all over Germany to enjoy the highlight of the fall season. The brewing cycle is completed for German beer at this time of the season and naturally this calls for a celebration. What better way to celebrate then with their own beer, and the Germans certainly love their beer.

As we got off the train we saw the most typical of all Oktober—fest scenes. Right in front of us was one of those famous pictures that I have seen on many beer commercials. Except this time I was not looking at a large billboard, but a real-life wagon being pulled by six Clydesdale horses, bigger than any I had ever seen in the commercials. They were just huge! I think that each of those six horses must have weighed one thousand pounds. These were the largest animals I have ever seen with the exception of elephants. Behind the horses were two men dressed in typical German outfits, and on the huge flatbed wagon was at least a half-dozen barrels of beer, also the biggest barrels I had ever seen.

At Oktoberfest everything appears to be extraordinarily large. We walked behind the wagon for while and then turned off to do a little sightseeing of this old city. We walked though the old town hall and went down to a little ratskeller for lunch. Bob introduced me to a famous German dish called Weiner Schnitzel. Since he made such a fuss about it, I decided to try it and it was delicious.
In the afternoon we visited the Siemens factory that was very modern and impressive. We toured their semiconductor plant that was as modern as any plant in the U.S.

At about four in the afternoon we went to the section of the city that is dedicated to the celebration of the Oktoberfest. During the year the area is a playing field where about six soccer matches take place at the same time. It was simply a gigantic playground. But now the city erects six huge tents each seating over one thousand joyous happy Germans. Inside are long straight tables with no other choice of beverage but German beer. We were escorted half way down the middle of the tent and were quite close to the bandstand where for the next six hours a variety of Bavarian bands entertained. The music was typically German. It was a scene that I will remember for a lifetime.
One of the most impressive people in this very impressive scene was the waitresses. Dressed in typical Bavarian skirts and aprons they, too, seemed extraordinarily large and had the biggest hands I ever saw. I think these waitresses were

chosen for the size of their hands. I watched them place five or six pitchers of beer in each of their "paws". Then, they brought them to their assigned area, and slid them down the long table to the designated receiver.

The drinking, singing and dancing went on throughout the night. Our visit was for just one night, but that was enough for us. Oktoberfest goes on for a week. I think that the Germans drink up all their profits during that week alone. Nevertheless, they certainly have a wonderful time and we did also.

11. Time Out for Germany

During our trips to Germany, our company often exhibited our Radar Warning Receivers at the annual Defense Electronic Show in Wiesbaden. The first time I was there in 1970 I was immediately impressed with this little town's neat and clean appearance. The comparison to the New York streets and subways marked up with terrible graffiti (this was during New York's 1970's graffiti phase), and the cleanliness of Wiesbaden was startling.

On the first evening after I arrived, I came in contact with my first "walking" street. I left a busy normal street crowded with cars, buses and taxis and I crossed over into the barricaded area, and it was like going into a new world. The idea of pedestrian streets without cars or taxis closed to vehicles blew my mind. What a wonderful idea! I thought. Why didn't we Americans think of this? The most dangerous of vehicles was a baby carriage or two wheelers and every once in a while a three-wheeler would roll by.

I remember crossing back and forth as I looked into store windows, thinking to myself, isn't it great not to worry about getting hit by a cab? In addition to the fact that there were no cars, buses or cabs I was in for another surprise. It was my first experience with street-side entertainment. Strolling musicians, mimes, and artists sitting on stools and painting willing subjects, also added to the ambiance of the city. What fun Wiesbaden was! After dinner at one of the many restaurants along the main street, Jim and I went back to our hotel for yet another surprise.

In Germany, the second half of a city's name tells one about the story of this city. "Baden" means "bath" in German. All over Germany, everywhere the Old Roman legions found hot water streaming out of underground springs, they established a city. For example, Baden Baden and, Wiesbaden have remained until modern times. In the lower level of our hotel, Nassauhof, we found a great pool that was converted from a hot spring. It was wonderful to go swimming and relax my tired muscles.

There were other interesting aspects of German towns that made them very different from American cities. The first park that I visited just outside of Wiesbaden gave me another surprise. As I walked through the park I saw piles of branches and leaves. They were obviously going to be picked up the next day. I walked into the park and suddenly realized that the entire park was raked to perfection. It looked like someone's private little garden. Whereas in the United States, parks are left more or less in their natural state, German parks are kept in a perfectly groomed state. Everything about Wiesbaden seemed to be neat and clean. Even the shops were kept immaculate and its merchandise was in perfect order.

On that first day, I went into a little shop that had some famous handmade Coo-Coo clocks. There were dozens of such clocks all over the walls. Each one set to the proper time, perfectly dusted and cleaned.

That day I bought the first of many Coo-Coo clocks that started my clock connection over the years. Since that day I have purchased one-day clocks, seven day clocks, clocks with single movements, clocks with multiple tones, and clocks that had rotating movements of all types. Each year I would buy a more complicated type to add to my collection. They still hang in my kitchen after more than a generation and surprisingly some still operate.

I have spent many days of my travels in Germany going from Munich to Bremerhaven; from Frankfurt-on-Main to Dresden; from Hamburg to Heidleburg; from Berlin to Hanover; but I remember best that first day walking through the center of Wiesbaden.

When we decided to take the trip to Munich in 2004 and enjoy a day at the Oktoberfest, we were told to be sure to get to the Frankfurt station on time, but we did not listen to that admonition too carefully. We thought German trains would be like New York trains out of Penn Station where one always has a few minutes leeway.

That cool and clear October morning we drove from Wiesbaden and arrived at the Frankfurt station to get the 8:00 A.M. express train to Munich. As I remember it, we neared the gate a moment or two before eight and we walked almost too casually up to the train doors. To our complete shock, at precisely eight o'clock the gate closed, and we found ourselves standing outside as the train pulled away.

We could not believe that a train would actually leave precisely at the instant they said they would. As a result of our mistrust, we caught the 9: 00 A.M. to Munich.

12. A Breath of Fresh Air "On The Road To The Black Forest"

During our 2004 visit to Germany, Lila and I decided to see the Black Forest, a little corner quietly nested between Germany, France, and Switzerland. Our plan was to rent a car at the airport and drive the fifty or so miles to the Spielweg Hotel in the little town of Munstertal on the edge of Germany's Black Forest. I had heard of the magnificent Black Forest from the time I had first visited Germany. Each year when I came to Wiesbaden to exhibit at the Defense Electronics Show, I always thought that some day I would be able to take a few extra days and go hiking in the forest. One year I took an extra day and went to Munich for the Oktoberfest. One year I was able to visit Heidelberg, that wonderful university town. Each of those holidays took but one day. To see the Black Forest would take at least three days and I was never able to sneak off for that amount of time. But now at last in retirement I would see this wonderful area of Germany.

When Lila and I arrived at the Eurocar rental company, they looked up my reservation and gave me the bad news that there was no car reserved for the Weisbergers, How could that be? I questioned. I knew my travel agent, Dix Hills Travel, would not have made an error and forgotten to make the reservation. I persisted. "There must be some mistake in your computer" I said. The agent returned to her computer, stared at the screen for endless minutes, and came back with a smile.

"The good news is, you have a Eurocar reserved for you." She said. The bad news is that it is in the Swiss part of the airport and you have to go to their car rental counter, about 300 meters away. Now who would have guessed there would be a French and Swiss Eurocar rental office in one airport. But there in this unusual corner of Europe there are a lot of unusual situations.

I told the car rental agent it was very difficult for me to get around so could I please get a French Eurocar instead of a Swiss Eurocar? I eventually lucked out and after she went back to her precious computer, she informed me that they could rent me a French car. Of course the instruction guide in the glove compartment is in French, she told us, whereas the Swiss car has a German instruction manual. I thought that over for a moment and smiled from ear to ear and told her it made no difference because I do not read either language. She gave me a slight smile and in her cute French accent said, "Yes I see what you mean".

After I got the car I spent about twenty minutes trying to get all the controls to function. Well, almost all. I could not get the automatically controlled rear view mirror to turn. No matter what button I pressed or what I knob I turned nothing would get those mirrors to reposition. I never drove a French-made Mercedes before and they must have hidden that control so only the French drivers could find it. I heard that some French do not like the Americans so this is probably how they get even. But I found out when I sat at an a certain angle relative to the steering wheel, I could use the mirror.

At last, Lila and I were off on the road to the Black Forest. I had a German map and a French map so I felt safe in finding my way to the little romantic village called Munstertal. I decided to take the slower road B-3, and not the Autobahn. As it turned out it was a good decision. It did not take over an hour and I was able to see the dozen or so little German towns along the way. The interesting fact was that we never did find out when we actually crossed over from France Switzerland and then to Germany. On the other hand maybe we never did get to Switzerland. What I suddenly realized that the signs had changed and I decided that sometime during the trip we where in Germany. On thinking back about the trip, it must have been when we crossed over a bridge with the Rhine River below that we were in Germany. The days of Border guards and stamped passports are gone, at least for this very civilized part of Europe. Of course, with the conversion to the Euro there seems very little concern what country you are in.

I drove for quite a while and the land was flat and rather boring. Then the terrain started to rise and with it my expectations for this land of beauty. Then Lila saw the sign for Bad Krosingen which is a little town before the little village of Staufen before the smaller village of Munstertal. With each smaller town the land became more and more beautiful. When we finally decided that this must be heaven on earth we saw the sign saying Munstertal. The suffix "tal "is German for valley. The word munster is an old way of saying cathedral or church.

The town stretches along a magnificent valley about six or seven miles long and it is broken up into three sections, the lower, middle and upper. During our six-day visit with our friend, Anemone and Bernd Achtnect and their daughter, Zoro, I drove the stretch from the lower part to the upper part a dozen or so times. Each time I made the trip I had to remember to keep my eyes on the road and not to stare out the side windows to see the hills and the lanes in this gorgeous valley. There are not many places on this earth, I decided, that were as beautifully scenic as this stretch of road. With only the few dozen homes along the way, there is plenty of open space to enjoy the absolutely gorgeous green hills which reminded me of the movie, "Sound of Music."

The cows and the sheep that live on these magnificent hills must be the luckiest in the world, I thought, one day, as I drove along the road. The fields on either side line the hills and have such healthy tall pines spread out among them, that one is tempted to look at them even though I kept my eyes on the road. As if that was not enough, anyone who felt the added need to communicate with the lord, there is a spectacular cathedral along the road between the upper and lower sections of the town.

One day Anemone and I walked inside this very beautiful cathedral. We walked quietly throughout it and then returned to the brilliant sunshine of the world of the Black Forest. I never would have suspected that such a little town would have such place of worship. It is called St. Trudpest. Every time I passed it, I felt its architectural beauty that seemed to go with the landscape, and so must the people, vacationers and residents alike who take the hike along this stretch of road. One other feeling that Lila experienced was the clean, fresh atmosphere that made one unusually conscious of the "taste of the air." After she made me conscious of it, I became aware of the wonderful air around us.

Now in New York, we take the air very much for granted and we usually accept the polluted air around us. Sometimes we curse the fumes when they get intolerable from the buses and the taxis trying to speed up to beat the traffic signals. If we are lucky enough to get a breath of fresh Central Park air between the hordes of cars speeding throughout the park to beat the traffic signals, we say, "doesn't the air smell good?" Of course relative to the pollution of the East River Drive or the speeding cars keeping up with the timed signals of First Avenue, Central Park is an oasis. Now all of a sudden Lila and I really came upon air that made our lungs say, "Oh! thank you, thank you, I needed this."

We sat out on our terrace at the Spielweg Hotel looking at the green hills above, uttering "this is a real breath of fresh air!"

13. Munstertal, A String of A Town

Our Plan was to stay in the town of Munstertal for approximately one week where we would experience the famous and very beautiful Schwarzwald (Black Forest).

The town is in a long very thin valley that stretches for about about six kilometers from what is called lower Munstertal to Upper Munstertal. The lower town is no more than three streets wide with a church and town hall in the center. The homes rest comfortably along the valley road. In the center the houses are rather close together. They are very well kept and as you drove along the narrow road one has the feeling of complete security and comfort. The "kinder" (children) ride their bicycles along the road and the seniors walk vigorously with their walking sticks along the roads that make up this string of a town. I thought of it as a string because it is so long and narrow. But the other feeling I had was that it is a happy town. The first day I arrived my friend, Bernd was giving a walking class to about twenty students. Now why would anyone have to take a walking class? I discovered that in the Black Forest walking is an art.

Each of his students is given a pair of walking sticks much like ski poles. They are taught how to hold them with their wrists and use them in the art of hill climbing. I watched as the class stood in front of Bernd's and Anemone's home that is also their business office. Not only do they teach walking but Bernd also gives physical massages.

Since walking is not my best subject, I had a massage from Bernd that was just wonderful. After my massage I drove to the upper section of Munstertal to our hotel, the Spielweg.

14. Experiencing the Black Forest

Maybe it was the clean air, maybe the beautiful hills and the peaceful valleys, but visiting this part of the world does wonders for your sensibilities. One day Lila and I walked down into an old silver mine known as Besuchsbergwerk. The mine has a very special feature—its air is considered to be the cleanest in the world. Many people with asthma go there to rejuvenate themselves. Although we did not reach all the way into the area where people take the special treatment, we did walk far enough into the mine to get the feeling of the cool clear air all around us. The mine is some 550 meters long, and Lila and I walked to the 120-meter mark.

At this point we stopped and pulled out our digital cameras and had lots of fun taking pictures in the depth of the mine. The mine is lit with small incandescent light bulbs and it was an exciting experience to be in a mine for our very first time. The cameras recorded our adventure down the depths of the mine. It was cool and dark but the air was definitely clear and clean. Our flash proved capable of giving the optics the necessary light. As we walked down the length of the mine, the pain in my back increased. I realized just how little distance I am able to walk now in 2004 at the age of 77. But I must keep on going. I am not going to stop experiencing fun and exciting places because of a pain in the back. I know that I can only do a sampling of what I was able to do even five years ago. I am not going to stop viewing the world that I love. I will keep on going no matter how little I can do. Even if I do just a little sampling, that will be a satisfying experience for me.

On another day my Black Forest friend, Anemone, took me to the highest the mountain in that area of the forest. We took the cable car to the top of Mount

Belchen. The car is one of those used during the ski season. It was comfortable and so very quiet as we were the only two into that car that day. In the center of the car are slits so that skiers can put their skis down into the holes and not have to take them off and then they got out of the cable car, they could immediately start skiing down. But for us that day, skiing was not the activity but rather sight-seeing of the valleys and the surrounding mountains on this beautiful autumn day. The cable cars took us to about 200 meters from the top. From there on, it was quite a hike to the very peak of Mount Belchen. Anemone and I began the trek to the top. We walked a while and then stopped to rest for a few minutes. It was rather hard for me. Then we started again, but in a short time I had to stop once more.

Then my mother's long remembered line came to me.

"What am I trying to prove, and who am I trying to prove it to?"

So I could not make it to the top. It was enough that I was there on this beautiful day with my good friend and companion. We then hiked back to the little lunch bar and had something to eat before taking the cable car back to the valley.

On the last day before leaving for the United States, the Weisberger and Acht-nich families took a scenic excursion in and around several towns of the Black Forest. First we went to Staufen, the town where Goethe wrote his famous stories about Dr. Faustus and the devil. I had not read them but I vowed I would when I got back home. The town is just like it was a century and a half ago. As we walked down the main street of Staufen the adults talked about poetry and the ancient castle up on the hill, while the Achtnich's little daughter, Zora, danced and played with her new gift. Lila brought Zora some new dolls from the United States. They were the kind of dolls Anemone and Zora had always dreamed of having. Zora immediately made a bonding relation with one of the dolls. It was a fairy doll with wings and a little white flower pinned to her dress. Zora shyly whispered to her mother in German. "I will name her White Rose," she said.

So Zora and White Rose played and danced in the streets of Staufen. She is a very independent seven-year-old and enjoys playing by herself in a world of fantasy. Almost immediately, she made up a game of hide and seek and she would hide White Rose in a shrub and try to find her. Then in German she would call to Anemone, her mother," Where is White Rose?"

Then answering her own query, she would shout gleefully "Oh! Here she is."

I did not have to understand German to watch this beautiful little, red-haired, girl at play.

The walking streets and the old buildings took one back to the Nineteenth Century. From the end of the street where the old gate once stood you can see the ancient castle built by the Romans two thousands years ago. All over Southern Germany are castles. The Romans built cities everywhere they would find hot springs. Those Romans knew the value of rejuvenation by taking hot baths.

From Staufen we drove to the town of Badenweiler where Anemone had lived when she was a young girl. Bernd, who was driving, pointed out the many little towns and villages along the way. When we reached Badenweiler we saw the scores of couples, young and old, walking along the streets, going to and from the famous spas and hot springs. The center of the town was crowded with old hotels and rooming houses where the Germans go on holiday.

After a while we came upon the little house at the end of a once tiny street where Anemone rode her bike and played with her friends when she was but five years old. She told us about the fun days of her youth in Badenweiler, we started the ride up the steep roads of the Black Forest. As we went higher and higher the road became narrow and narrower. On one side the mountains closed in, rising sharply upward. On the other side of the road was a steep decline to the valley below. The beauty everywhere was breathtaking. It reminded Lila and I of the drive in Colorado up to the top of Pikes Peak.

Finally we reached the restaurant to enjoy lunch and the scenery. As we arrived at the top of the mountain the clouds thickened and the air was filled with moisture. One did not have to be a meteorologist to know it was about to rain. But before we went inside, Anemone, Bernd and even Zora, gave Lila and I a briefing on the different types of edible plants that existed everywhere in the Black Forest. We were absolutely amazed how many plants and berries they knew and could identify. Each of them would bend down and pick up a leaf or a berry, telling us, which to eat and which were not edible. It was clear that this family would never starve if they were lost in the woods. I thought to myself, if I were lost in the United States, I would just call AAA. Although in my scouting days, sixty years ago, I did know about many plants and flowers. Unfortunately, I have long since forgotten how to survive in the wilderness.

We went inside the restaurant on the top of the mountain and had a typical German afternoon dinner. Bernd and I had Wiener schnitzel. Anemone and Zora shared a platter of cheese and sausages. Lila stuck with the very American ice cream pops; two of them. So our trip to Europe, France, Germany and the Black Forest had come to an end.

Mt. Belchen, Black Forest, Germany,

15. More Than Just a Book Fair

I never visited the Frankfurt Book Fair. The closest I came physically was taking a sightseeing trip to this now modern city a decade ago. But when I read about it in the New York Times and emailed it to my friend, Anemone in Germany, I asked her if she had ever been there. I received such a very enthusiastic response that I thought you'd like to hear about it too. Here is her story.

"Frankfurt book fair is much more than just a presentation of books and publishing houses, more than just a platform for editors, publisher, writers and booksellers to connect. It is all that, but it is also a great cultural event—and as a visitor, you have to think about a priority plan to plow your way through all those amazing waves and vibes, cause there's no way you can see or hear or experience them all (that, or just drifting around—but then, you might miss the most interesting events and people by a just few minutes or meters).

I have been there as an editor's assistant, as a bookseller and during the last years, as a visitor, and each time it has been very stimulating.

When my job for a publishing house brought me there, I had to make contact with potential international license partners and present our books and authors to them, and then as a bookseller, I was responsible for the profile of the store and had to check books and purchase conditions. Although I enjoyed the work, it was stressful. As a visitor, however, you're free to listen to whatever you want to, check in wherever you feel like it, spend time at whatever reading or exhibition or discussion that calls to you. I greatly enjoyed that.

In the numerous big halls, the publishing houses have their booths (though the term booth sounds much too small for the often huge literature auditoriums they have built). There, you can look at and into thousands of books, learn about their background, meet authors, illustrators and editors, and often also listen to readings and discussions. On the huge patio formed in the center of the halls, are several tents and bungalows. There is a reading tent, for instance, where famous and not-so-famous authors read from their books, It's nonstop reading, and you can enter any time, have a coffee and sit down in the morning sun or twilight and listen.

In the bungalows and other tents, the events and exhibitions of the "guest country" are taking place (there is a different country every year that is the 'main topic' of the fair, which presents itself through its literature and culture). One year I was there, it was Russia, the year before that Lithuania. This year it is the Arabic countries and next year, it will be Korea. There, you can find readings, art shows, dance, performances, discussions, exhibitions and more. The literature of the guest country (and more background info about its culture) can be found in a building called the forum, where many rooms for movies and readings and discussions about that topic are also provided.

I've seen a wonderful Algerian black-and-white movie there, for instance, talked for quite a while with a representative of the library of Alexandria (what an amazing building!), listened to a hot discussion among an Iraqi, a Syrian and an Egyptian on a platform and have seen an amazing virtual nine-screen interactive presentation of ancient Egypt.

Afterwards, I went out to the patio again, where I ran into a wonderful xylophone player (a New York born Jew who now lives in Jerusalem. The artistic dance of his hands on the xylophone was amazing and lured the most beautiful sounds out of his instrument. Then I went to the literature tent and heard some young 'neo-beat' authors read from their works. I entered one of the pavilions where four Arab men read their poetry (we got translation headphones, and I switched between the translation and the originals to hear the sound and rhythm of their voices). Afterwards, I discovered a wild and wonderful Egyptian dance show in another bungalow.

Then I went to the art exhibition bungalow. There was beautiful modern art (the paintings in those warm and beautiful earthy colors), ancient art and crafts from different Arabic countries, and a wonderful exhibition of Yemenite poetry rugs. And more…there was so much more." and the following:

Signed: Anemone Achtnich

Munstertal, Germany

I am looking forward to go there myself some day. It seems like an extremely interesting and inspiring event.

ICELAND

16: Worth a Trip From Anywhere

My most recent trip to the Arctic was a van tour around Iceland with my friend, Marty. It was the middle of May, 1999 when eight of us piled into a four-wheel drive van to visit this little known-about island in the middle of the Atlantic Ocean. We were a variety of travelers from Australia, Sweden and the United States, and, our guide, Ari, was Icelandic.

When we arrived, so did spring and it was an exciting time to visit the place. Flowers were beginning to bloom and trees were beginning to bud after a hard winter's sleep. The countryside is an interesting combination of snow, ice, mud and volcanic lava. Right at the beginning, the trip was almost a disaster for Marty and me. Our first night in Reykjavik was spent in a little motel. Our plan was to leave early in order to circumnavigate the island in about one week. I woke up in the middle of the night with a medical emergency, and Ari had to take me to the Reykjavik Hospital for treatment. It was a modern place with great doctors and nurses. I discovered that Icelandic doctors are called by their first name and the Doctor prefix.

I felt very badly that Marty would possibly miss this trip of a lifetime, but I did not have any choice. Surprisingly, the doctor gave me a medicine that cured my problem. The next day we flew to the first stop of the trip to meet the group at the airport, and our trip was saved.

The little island has some of the most varied and interesting earthly phenomenon I have ever encountered. For example there are geysers like those found in Western United States and in Rotorua in New Zealand. As a matter of fact the word "geyser comes from the name of an Icelander who first recognized the phenomenon of spouting superheated water coming from deep within the earth.

The sulfur fields in Lake Myvaten are very healthy to swim in. One fine day we visited a lake about two miles across that has magnificent chunks of ice that float around in a never-ending cycle. Our skipper pulled up to several of these mini-bergs varying from two to ten feet in beautiful and interesting shapes and with an ice hammer, broke off pieces for us to suck on. As we were enjoying the cold, he informed us that the ice we were licking was over 600 years old but tasted fresh to me.

Iceland is certainly full of very interesting physical phenomenon. One day we came upon a beautiful waterfall that seemed to arise out of nowhere. There were farms all around and right in the middle was this gorgeous one hundred foot waterfall. We hiked around and under it for an hour.

The beauty of Iceland is everywhere. A few miles away we came upon what is said to be the smallest church in the world. Only six of us could enter at a time. It had just two benches and one window, but Icelanders said that God is everywhere. Then we headed for the sulfur fields that were beyond magnificent. The fields were bubbling columns of magnificent yellow, red, and brown streams of sulfur coming from inside our planet that form dozens of little sulfur mounts about five or six feet high. The one unpleasant part of the sulfur fields was the odor. The only way to describe it was that they smelled like rotten eggs. But then again you cannot have it all.

One highlight of the trip was to drive up to the top of a glacier that was the highest point on the entire island. The tour plan was to use the four-wheel nine-passenger vehicle to drive up to the little shack at an altitude of 1500 feet. Then we were to transfer to snowmobiles, which are two passenger little buggies that would take us the rest of the way to the glacier's top. However when we actually arrived at the shack there were already six other tourists waiting for their snowmobiles to take them up. There were two each of Germans, Norwegian, and Swedes and with the six of us there was a total of twelve tourists looking forward to making it to the highest point of Iceland. Now the clouds had begun to grow heavier and the slight drizzle had changed to snow. I thought to myself "how strange to have snow in summer." But in the arctic anything can happen.

Our tour guide, Ari, and the twelve of us waited for the other tour guide to return in his snowmobiles and report the conditions at the top. While we waited we idly passed the time by looking out the window and talking about whether or not we should go.

The Germans and Norwegians said we should go on, but we Americans, and the Swedes said to turn back. In a little while the Icelandic guide came in. He had been up to the top in his snowmobile and informed us that the weather was just too bad to continue further. We never made it to the top.

Although small in size, Iceland has the most varied geological phenomenon to be seen anywhere. Besides the ice fields, lakes, glaciers, geysers, sulfur fields, and falls, it has many volcanoes that were active as recent as ten years ago. Everyday was an experience and I would recommend taking a trip to Iceland for anyone who loves our planet.

In the past thirty or forty years much progress has been made to use the natural heat from underground for developing hot houses to grow fruits and vegetables. There are towns that are entirely heated by the water coming from the underground hot water springs. This brings up the sad element in our environmental history in that over the past three hundred years, there has been the near destruction of the Icelandic tree forests. In the last four or five centuries all the lumber was used for homebuilding and making fires. When it was already too late, the Icelanders realized that they would have no more wood. They started a tree-growing project, and planted over fifty million little saplings like the Israeli did in Israel. After thirty or forty years they realized that it would take hundreds of years to grow back their forests. They are very saddened about this, but are trying to make up for it in others ways, like using their hot water asset to heat schools and homes and hot houses. I saw an entire banana plantation within a hot house. It seemed so strange to see bananas growing indoors, and snow on the ground right outside the door.

Besides the very special geographic conditions in Iceland, the characteristics of its people are very interesting. How so, you say?

Let me tell you a few ways. For one thing Icelanders still do not use last names. They use their first name and their father's first name with the word "son" following it. In the case of a girl, she uses her first name and her father's first name followed by her relationship to him, daughter, "dottur" in Icelandic. For example, my name in Iceland would be Eugene Jacobson (son of Jacob). My wife's name would be Lila Samueldottur (daughter of Samuel).

Other fun facts about the Icelandic people:
They hardly ever borrow money even for a mortgage. They don't think it is good practice to do that. They never honk their horns and think that it is very bad manners does to do so. One day during the trip, we sat behind another car for what seemed like an hour to us high-speed Americans, and our guide did not honk his horn.

They indeed have interesting personalities. As I left Reykjavik at the end of our trip I realized what a wonderful place I had just visited. It has been ten years since I visited that little island in the Arctic. During that time I have met but two people who have traveled to this remote place. One lady whose family came from the island and who goes back every few years to refresh her spirit and relationships, and another, a young woman world traveler, who went there on vacation. Both of them felt as I do, that Iceland is one of the most beautiful, exciting and most unique places on earth.

For travelers who believe that they have seen the world my advice is to see Iceland. It is worth the trip from anywhere.

17. A Prayer For Bergen

My first introduction to Bergen, Norway was in a very unusual way. It was by means of South Korea and London. Now how can someone be introduced to a village along the coast of Northern Europe by means of a country on the very opposite side of the planet? I must admit some of my introductions are very unusual. Here is the story.

Our company had been trying to sell a very sophisticated electronic system to the South Korean oceanographic office for many months during the 1980's. The sonar system which is called Seabeam (See Birth of Seabeam In Volume Two of my book, Lazarus) uses multi-beam projectors and hydrophones to map the ocean floor. Although we originally made the system for the U. S. Navy, subsequently we received permission to sell the system to other countries such as France, Australia, and Japan. Prior to the development of Seabeam, only single beam systems were used by countries, and it took much more time and a lot of trail and error on the part of a cartographer, to plot the ocean floor. With the invention of Seabeam, maps were made in real-time as ships would sail through the oceans.

As South Korea became interested in the natural resources such as oil, gas and precious minerals lying under their coastal sea floors, they began to realize they too needed such a system. Over a period of two years they contacted us requesting information and a technical proposal. During that time, several trips were made by Don White, our General Manager, Undersea Systems Division, and other staff members to convenience them of the benefits of having such a system.

We hired a representative, Key Young Chung in Seoul to help us sell the system. It was a long slow process however. But finally their Oceanographic Office made up its mind. One of the complications of using Seabeam, however, was that a special ship with a broad hull was needed to mount the many projectors and hydrophones which were part of the multibeam sonar system. The Koreans did not have a ship with the proper configuration to mount our system. So a ship had to be designed and ultimately built to mount the system. Their oceanographic office in Inchon, South Korea, spent more than six months designing such a ship. At last the design was complete, the ship was ready for bid and shipyards around the world were asked to submit their proposals. I followed the progress of the program because the selling of a Seabeam system, a high value item, was a major project. On one occasion Don White and I went to South Korea, met with our rep. Key Young Chung and visited oceanographic staff in Inchon.

During our visit we were assured that they intended to buy our system and that it was just a matter of time before they had all the final approvals. After the visit I felt confident we would get the program and that probably a modern South Korean company would get the shipbuilding contract, although it was possible that a Japanese shipyard might also get it.

I was surprised to hear one day that a little Norwegian shipyard out of Bergen Norway was chosen. I had never even heard of Bergen before. Finally at long last we received the contract for the South Korean Seabeam and the program was under way. About nine months later I had the opportunity to go to the United Kingdom to visit the Royal Air Force and follow the progress of a Radar Warning Receiver program.

I often tried to review several projects when I traveled overseas to make such a trip worth the effort. So on that occasion I decided to meet Don White in Bergen, Norway, to follow up on the progress of the South Korean shipbuilding program. One of my management styles was to keep in contact with all elements of major programs. To me there was nothing like touching and feeling a program to get a better understanding of its progress. Although we were not responsible for the ship—building portion of the project, the ship had to be built in order for our Seabeam system to get installed. Since I was only an hour's flight away, I decided to see the progress first hand. I met Don in a small Bergen hotel on the evening before my inspection. It was summer and the sun did not set until almost eleven o'clock, so we spent an hour walking around the little town.

It was a pretty place with many walking streets, and small shops open for tourists until late into the night. I always enjoyed walking around little European towns. Bergen was neat and clean and my first reaction to it was very positive. The next morning we walked through the college and over the hills to the ship building area. I was surprised there were so many vessels being built and over-hauled along the riverfront. The place was as busy as a beehive. At last we arrived at the South Korean vessel and I was very happy to see that the ship was almost complete. Don and I walked throughout the ship and then under the hull. From the perspective of a ship nothing seems so huge as walking under a ship in dry dock. The projectors and hydrophones, which are part of the Seabeam system, were already installed.

As I walked under the ship I got the feeling of clostrophobia. The thought flashes through my mind. What happens if the wooden blocks holding up the ship, would suddenly give way. Obviously one would get crushed like an ant. But of course such an accident has never taken place. The thought quickly left my mind as I proceeded with the inspection.

I have been in other shipyards throughout the USA but this was my first experience visiting a European shipyard. They are very different than American shipyards. There was no mass production. Every portion of the ship was build by hand. Each worker was given his part of the ship to build. He had his little box of carpentry tools and he used them with great tender love and care. I imagine it would have been done that same way when sailing ships were built. I could not believe that the price for building a ship that way would have been less than a modern shipyard. But there it was! This little company had under-bid all the big Oriental shipyards. When I finished my inspection I was tremendously impressed that old-fashioned hard work existed somewhere in the world. In addition to their industry and drive, I was impressed with the personality of these Scandinavians. I loved their smiling ways and their very nice dispositions.

When we left the shipyard, Don and I walked around this very pretty little town and found the people to be friendly, going out of their way to show us a wonderful time. I did not meet a single Norwegian who did not speak English and help us in every way possible. One evening we went to an Edvard Greig concert and had a great time listening to the music of this famous son of Norway. Three days later I headed home, really happy that I had taken that one-hour flight from London.

Six years later Lila and I spent ten days on the exploration ship, Polaris, traveling throughout the islands of Spitzbergen about six hundred miles north of Norway's mainland. At the conclusion of that trip we sailed down the coast and into the many fjords of this magnificent country before arriving at Bergen. There are not many countries in the world that are prettier than Norway. One fjord, the Sagafjord, is over one hundred miles long. At end of it we took a bus up into the mountains for a spectacular view. At the end of the bus route we walked up the mountains and looked down into the fjord to see our little ship that looked like a toy compared to the mountains on either side. The little villages throughout the mountains going down to the river all around us are just spectacular. On one occasion we left the bus and hiked down through several little towns and finally arrived back at the Polaris.

We took a bus trip through a mountain road and our guide told us a joke that is worth repeating. The roads are very narrow and the hairpin turns are absolutely scary.

The story is as follows: A Bergen priest and a fjoyd bus driver died and went to heaven. The two of them were waiting for St. Peter to let them in. Saint Peter came to the gate, saw the bus driver and immediately let him in. An hour later the priest was still waiting to get through the gates and he asked St. Peter why he had to wait so long. The Priest complained. "You let the tour guide in immediately, why not me? After all I was the Priest of Bergen and he was only a tour guide in the mountains around the fjords of Norway." St Peter said, "When you conducted your prayer services in Bergen all the parishioners fell asleep. But when the tour guide took his bus around the hairpin turns throughout the mountains, down and up those treacherous turns, all the tourists prayed and called out, "Oh! God Oh! God, please get us out of here alive."(See "Exciting Spitzbergen" in my first book The Chinese Walking Stick)

IRELAND

18. A Relaxed and Friendly Country

After I became President of the Government Systems Group, the Vice President of Finance suggested to me that there was a very interesting management-training course given by a provocative Management Consultant named Walter Mahler. He had from ten to fifteen executives in his courses at each session. Each course consisted of a one-week seminar four times a year and for two consecutive years. The entire two-year program was quite expensive (cost $12,000) and he was so well thought of that there was a one-year waiting list. The courses were typically given in various cities around the U. S. usually favoring the cities where the executives were living. Typically, no sessions were given overseas.

So just how did we get to Ireland for the one week of our course? I signed up for one of Walt Mahler's eight one-week sessions spaced over two years and as a dividend had a wonderful trip around the very historic country of Ireland. My fellow students were from all over the country and from some of the most prestigious companies in the business world—General Electric, Dupont, Sara Lee,

Chase Bank and at least a half-dozen others. Although we were all high-level executives from general managers on up, we all liked to enjoy the time away from the books and lectures.

One of the most important characteristics about executives is that we are well-balanced people, believing in the rule of "All work and no play make Jack a dull boy." We were by no means dull boys. We loved to go out after the sessions and have a great dinner or participate in some very special activity.

Since we came from all over the United States when we met the first time Walter Mahler asked us to think about future locations for other seminars. Walt had the first seminar very close to his headquarters in New Jersey. Many of the executive headquarters were located in New York City as was General Instrument so most of us were very familiar with the big city. One evening during that first week's session we went to Atlantic City and gambled the night away.

The first week's program was about personnel training. Walt was a very illustrious and exciting teacher and the week flew by and before we knew it we were saying, "See you next quarter".

We sat around the table late the final evening picking various locations for the remaining seven weeks of seminars; California, Texas, Florida, Colorado, South Carolina and a dozen others were suggested. We agreed on the next six locations and Dr. Mahler's staff would choose the actual resorts. As we were about to choose the final location, an executive who was manager of a drug company in Dublin, Ireland spoke up. He suggested that we go to Ireland for the last week's seminar. He argued on the basis that he had to travel to the United States seven times, why not give him a break and have the last seminars in Ireland. It seemed logical to us although the airfare was so much more going to Europe. Surprisingly none of us had ever been to Ireland so we thought it would be a great way to visit another country.

Walt Mahler also agreed and the last week's seminar was chosen to be Ireland. Dr. Mahler said he would find an interesting place to spend the week. One year and a half went by and every three months we visited another exciting hotel or resort center. Walt's secretary had a great ability to pick wonderful places to hold these seminars. The resort outside of San Diego was a real horse ranch. We even had time to do some horseback riding. In Florida we went to a resort outside of Jacksonville, and we found time to do a lot of swimming and snorkeling when the rest of the country was in a deep freeze. In South Carolina the hotel was just a few miles outside of Charleston and we spent one evening taking a horse and buggy ride through the old city concluding with a great southern dinner in an old plantation. The week in San Antonio, Texas gave us the opportunity to see the

Alamo National Monument and staying at a luxurious condominium. In Denver we did some fun mountain climbing outside of Boulder on the day after the seminar ended.

During the year we received a notice from Dr, Mahler's office that the last seminar 's location had finally been chosen. In fact it would be held in an Irish castle called Dromoland in the county of Galway. We were also sent notices about highlights of Ireland. For nights I went to sleep reading about this fascinating and wonderful country. During the last ten years I must have gone to Europe one dozen times mostly to see electronic exhibitions but Ireland was not one of the countries I had seen or for that matter had not thought about visiting. Now suddenly Ireland was on the visiting map for me. Where was the Blarney Stone? Was Ring of Kerry worth seeing? Could we have time to see the Cliffs of Mohar?

The last seminar was scheduled for June, a wonderful time of year, I thought, for such a visit. Even luckier, it was set for the end of June so Lila would not miss too many days of her school semester if she accompanied me. Happily she agreed to go, although it turned out to be an unpleasant time for her.

Finally the day arrived and we flew off to Dublin in fine spirits. We stayed in a small hotel in the center of the city, the kind of hotel that James Joyce wrote about in Ulysses and spent days walking around the city including a visit to the famous Dublin University where the Book of Kells is housed. We had such wonderful and exciting days in that beautiful and historic city.

On our last evening Lila and I were sitting in a bar on O'Connell Street in the center of Dublin and began talking to two friendly young men.

"Wh're you from?" asks one of them.

"We're from New York," I answered, trying to hide my New York accent.

I continued the conversation with these very nice looking guys. "Where are you guys from?" I asked.

With a deep Irish brogue, the tall one answers, "We're from Northern Island." Then he questions me, "Have you ever been to Northern Island?"

"No, I haven't" I said. "We have only been here in the southern part of the republic and it's very beautiful."

With a bright smile he said, "If you think this is beautiful you should go up North."

Although the fighting had been over for more than a year by then, I hesitantly said, "I do not think that it is too safe."

Then the tall one says to his friend, with a hearty laugh and his deep brogue "Can you believe it? This guy is from New York and he is afraid to go to Northern Island?"

They both howled.

One day we decided to visit the Dublin Race Course. We a walked to the bus stop in the center of the city found the number of the bus going that way. It was jammed with people going to the races but at last we were able to get a seat in the rear. One characteristic the Irish have is that they are friendly and love to gab. Almost as soon as we sat down the man next to us started to converse. The usual conversation proceeded, "Where do ya come from?" What do you do?"

I asked him the similar type of question.

Before I knew it he was telling me his whole life story. He is employed in an office as a manager. He works very hard and it is a stressful job. He loves to take a day off, now and then, to get away from it all. Then he used the phrase that has stuck with me for lo these ten years. "Today is one of those days which I call a soft day."

I had never heard that expression before—"A Soft Day".

But after I thought about it—a day off—it made sense. The phrase stuck with me these twenty–odd years.

Sitting there I began to daydream about a day away from the trials and tribulations of my busy office scene. Being out in the fresh air, walking along the dirt road of a little Irish town with a warm breeze blowing my hair, I feel totally relaxed. My Irish tweed jacket is almost too warm for the first days of spring. My walking stick permits me to keep up a brisk pace. Then before I know it I am several kilometers from home. I stop at a local pub for a thirst quenching ale. "Tis a wondris day! A Soft Day to be sure," I mutter to myself. Then my daydream ends. I came to the conclusion that the Irish know how to relax.

The bus driver announces the race course and almost every sole on the bus gets out on the dirt road and heads for the large stadium about two hundred yards away, The road ends in about five minutes and we are walking in a field of tall grass. We walk much slower then the others and before we know it we are alone walking across this huge farm. We see several sheep grazing in the field. They do not concern us however because they are one of the most passive animals on earth. All of a sudden Lila starts sneezing a bit and says, "I think I am getting a cold. Neither of us is concerned.

We arrive at the racecourse and pay a shilling or two to get in. We spent several fun-filled hours watching race after race of some or the best Irish-bred horses in the country. I do not remember whether or not I won but I remember it was just a fun day.

As the sun begins to set we start out for Dublin and our hotel.

It was much harder to find our way to the bus stop however because everyone seemed to be going in different directions.

Finally we found a paved road, but by now Lila's cold had gotten much worse and she was very uncomfortable.

The next day our rented car would be ready and we were scheduled to drive around the country in a clock-wise direction ending up on the west side of the Island at Dromoland Castle. I had all sorts of books and maps ready to take this trip, but unhappily, Lila was not well. She was sneezing and blowing her nose almost continually now. She appeared to have a very bad cold.

But suddenly it dawned on us that it was not a cold at all but probably a severe allergic reaction to Ireland's very lush countryside. As we drove to little cities, like Waterford and Cork and attempted to visit the glass factories and sweater mills she was very uncomfortable. Finally in Cork we made an appointment with a local doctor. He verified that she was indeed allergic to the greenery of Ireland and gave her pills to reduce her reaction. Unfortunately the pills caused her to be very sleepy and she was drowsy for much of the next four days as we drove around one of the most beautiful sections of Ireland called the Ring of Kerry.

Around this southwestern corner of the country is a magnificent countryside surrounded by bays and coves. We stopped off at parks, souvenirs shops and little beaches throughout this pretty little section of Ireland. In the evening we stayed at a bread-and-breakfast Inn and had a delicious Irish stew dinner. In the morning we headed North to Shannon. I was a little confused about the direction to the ferryboat and asked a local for directions. Again, I experienced Irish hospitality and friendliness. I pulled out my map and showed the young man my concern. He then spent at least fifteen minutes jabbering away, showing me every road and turn I should take to reach the Dromoland Castle. I could not stop this friendly guy from talking. When he finished I was more confused than ever and anxious to get away. But I did find my way to the ferry-boat I needed to take. At last in the distance we could see the magnificent towers and the gray structure of Dromoland.

Since this was the first time the wives were invited to a Mahler seminar, the first activity was an evening introduction dinner. The wives got along very well and during the next week they went around the country sightseeing. Lila did not participate very much because the pills were still making her drowsy. At the first dinner we were hit with a surprise.

The executive from the drug company who encouraged us to have the final seminars in Ireland about eighteen months ago, was unexpectedly absent. When we asked Dr. Mahler where he was, we were told that he had been transferred back to his company's home office in Kansas and would not be joining the seminar this week. At the end of the week I wrote him a letter thanking him for inviting us to Ireland. It was the one and only trip I ever took because of someone else's desire. I told him how happy I was for his invitation and that I'd never met more friendly people than the Irish.

UNITED KINGDOM

19. "Yes, Gene, where are our seats?"

I have not written much about England in the past as I have about other countries so I felt it was now time to tell some stories about this fabulous country. Just as I spent a lot of time in Germany starting with the Electronics Shows, I began to visit England starting with the Farnboro Air Shows. Farnboro is a little town about 30 miles from London, but once every two years it becomes a crowded city with thousands and thousands of people who come to see exciting air demonstrations and the latest in new aircraft. The Farnboro Air Show alternates with the Paris Air Show on a yearly basis to demonstrate the latest in electronics and aircraft. When the show was in England we would stay in London mostly at the Hilton Hyde Park across from the park of the same name. The park is very much like Central Park even down to the horse and buggies. However, there is one aspect that is very different. In a corner of the park near Oxford every Sunday morning, speakers would stand on soapboxes and talk about whatever is on their minds. Extremely vocal audiences from ten to several hundred would express their opinions sometimes in favor, but often to the contrary. It is an exciting time and often the "bobbies" (English Police) have to break up the over–exuberant groups.

The place is appropriately called Speaker's Corner and to spend an hour or two listening to all sides of a discussion is a real fun experience. When I was there the last time in 1980, there must have been twenty people standing on their boxes talking on such diverse subjects as the break up of the House of Lords or the elimination of the Indian immigration. It sure gave the commoners a chance to get things "off their chests." The park is a great place to walk around on a Sunday morning or row down the serpentine. (a snake-like) river in the center of the park. After a week's work standing on your feet at the Air Show, this was a very pleasant get-away experience, indeed.

Speaking of get-a-ways, once I took a bus to Stonehenge a couple of hours from London and then went on to Bath. These two locations have extremely ancient histories which until then I knew little about—always something new to learn about, I say.

Stonehenge must be at least 4000 years old. It is a circle of huge stones which has a variety of religious significances. It is amazing how these stones must have been moved without any tools. It is very surprising to think of the ancient Druids roaming the hills of this ancient land and praying to a variety of gods.

Even though Stonehenge is impressive it does not hold a candle to the Pyramids of Egypt constructed in about 4500 B.C. When one compares them to the Pyramids they are not much more than tinker toys, but nevertheless they do have quite a history.

Somewhere half way between present times and the days of Stonehenge, the Roman baths were built for the relaxation and entertainment of the invading forces from Rome. Built out of stone and with magnificent carvings they were used by the Romans for fun and enjoyment. These baths were great places for the warriors from central Europe. Every place that the Romans visited was a place where baths were built. As a matter of fact many of the cities all over Europe such as Wiesbaden, Bad Hamburg and Baden Baden were all cities named for the baths that were constructed there. I enjoyed the baths that are in the basements of many of the hotels such as, the Nassauhof in Wiesbaden, Germany. The Romans enjoyed the baths and so did I. It was amazing for me to visit the same baths in the city of Bath that the Romans themselves used. It is well worth a visit.

One day on another trip to England, Lila and I were visited Stratford–on Avon, the home of the great Bard. In the afternoon we visited Shakespeare's thatched-roof cottage with its fireplace and little bedrooms where he lived some four hundred years ago. Of course the highlight of the trip would be seeing a performance of one of his plays. I went to the box office to obtain tickets for that evening's performance. We were sadly told that every seat in the theater was sold out. I could not believe it. I thought we would be the only visitors to Stratford that week. I saw Lila's disappointment when I told her but promised we would get in somehow. In the evening we mingled with the crowds and I felt lucky that we would be able to get inside with no difficulty and so it was—we just walked in and found a seat. We had to move around as people came to claim the seats we were using. As the time for the performance drew near, every seat in the theater was occupied and we ended up with no place to sit. When the curtain went up, I said to Lila, "lets just sit on the steps and nobody will notice us."

The play began and we were happily watching it for about ten minutes. I thought we would be okay. Then an usher came to Lila and asked, "Where are your seats?"

At that moment Lila looked helplessly at me and said the line that I will remember always. Not knowing what to say, she responded, "Yes, Gene, where are our seats?"

We quietly left the theater and bid good-bye to Stratford.

There are so many places to visit in both England and Ireland it is difficult to choose which one to write about. Two places of special beauty in Ireland that I would recommend are the Ring of Kerry in the Southwest corner of this pretty land and the Cliffs of Mohar on the west coast of the country. The Ring is full of nooks and crannies of shear beauty. As you drive through the area there are dozens of little places to visit. To hike across a stream or up a hill or to shop for an Irish woolen sweater or a tweed jacket is such great fun. It is a side trip well worth taking.

Then there are the Cliffs! There are little bread and board places to spend a night on the way to the Cliffs. It is thrilling to look down at the ocean below and see the waves spraying the steep cliffs almost up to your feet. It is absolutely magnificent to walk along the ridge and look down at the cliffs from many different angles. One can say that the cliffs are half the Grand Canyon. That may be an overstatement but stopping off there is certainly worth a visit.

20. The Falkland's Coincidence

In the late fall of 1999, Marty and I walked off the ship onto the Falkland Islands in the little harbor of Port Stanley. We were five hundred miles from the coast of South America in one of the smallest inhabited islands in the Atlantic. We had been cruising from Buenos Aries, Argentina around the tip of South America and up the coast of Chile to Valparaiso. There was never much interest in the Falklands until 1981 when the Argentina Navy invaded the place. The idea was that Argentina wanted the islands to explore for oil and they, the Argentina generals, thought that the English Prime Minister, Margaret Thatcher, was too busy with her domestic problems at home in England to care. But of course they were wrong and the British sent an armada to the Islands and without any warfare took them back.

There are only about 2500 people living in Port Stanley and only about twice that number living in the entire islands. There was many more sheep and penguins living there. We tourists added almost 800 people to Port Stanley that autumn day. Typically Marty and I did not take a formal scheduled island tour but just wandered off the ship and into the town. At the edge of the first street there was a pretty lady in her forties standing by a car. She came up to us asking if we wanted to take a tour. Before we knew it a group of us were on our way to the penguin's hatchery where hundreds of penguins were living a comfortable life at least as well as the humans.

Marty and I hiked all over the place taking loads of pictures of these little chin-striped or spaghetti penguins as they are called. But this story is not about penguins but about people. Our guide was an outgoing lady and before we knew it she was telling us about her life in Port Stanley. She had been living on Stanley for over ten years. She told us that she had a husband and two sons and that her husband, Phil, had a little stamp shop just a few blocks from the port. (Every street is just a few blocks from the port) Since I am an avid stamp collector, I decided to walk to Phil's shop. Marty and I had no trouble finding it and we struck up a conversation as soon as we arrived.

Phil, a gregarious gentleman from England, told us his life story before we bought single stamp. He was a teacher in a private school outside of Liverpool and became bored with it. One day he looked at an advertisement in the local newspaper that said a school in the Falklands was looking for a schoolmaster. He decided to apply for the job. Before he knew it he was winging his way to the little town of Port Stanley and was teaching history and English in the only school there. He soon had a little house and made friends with the locals.

One day a friend told him that a tour group was coming for a week from the United States. Now you must know that Port Stanley is a tiny place with no hotels or boarding houses. The visitors who were coming would have to be put up somewhere. They found rooms for the visitors but there was no room for the guide. The man making the arrangements asked Phil if he would have a room for the guide. Although he had not as yet met the guide, Phil thought for a moment and then said, yes.

The day that the group arrived the guide came up the road to Phil's house. To Phil's surprise it was a nice young lady, not a gentleman. Phil said to her that he was surprised that she was a "she" and not a "he" Then he said, "You can stay so long as there is no trouble." There was no trouble. The young guide from Chicago stayed for the week and lots more. Before long Phil and Judy were married and have lived in the Falklands all this time

When I got back to the states, I told my travel agent about my visit to the Falklands and all about my guide and her husband and how they met. Coincidently, my travel agents Roberta and her husband, Harold, were booked to take a cruise around the tip of South America and they too were stopping off at Port Stanley.

When they arrived at the Port they recognized the lady guide standing at the corner of the pier. They went up to her and started to tell her all about <u>her</u> life. She was shocked that someone who just got off the ship knew all about her. After their tour to the penguins they told her that when I came back from my visit I told them about her and how she met her husband. She was relieved it was only a word-of-mouth coincidence and not that the whole outside world knew all about her.

3

Marco's Travels

1. Training In China

During our two trips to China, one in the heat of summer in 1988 and one in the beauty of October of 1994, Lila and I had occasion to take two train rides. On our first trip we went from Shanghai to Nanjing in the heat of summer. We arrived at the train station as the conductor was opening every window, which told us in no uncertain words that our cars were without air conditioning. Not only was it sweltering hot but the cars were dusty beyond belief. Except for our American group of about twenty, everyone else in the train was Oriental. The Chinese were used to the heat and accepted it but we Americans walked around the car in a high state of discomfort and let our discomfort be known. The complaints never ended for the entire trip.

The train started out shortly after we arrived. As we left the Shanghai station I expected that, as we traveled the air could cool off a bit. But no such luck. The air was so hot and sticky it was actually hard to breath. After a while a little woman came around selling, of all things, hot cups of coffee.

I think the coffee was supposed to cool me off, but it did not work. I actually felt hotter. The coffee did provide liquid so I perspired more, which probably did tend to cool one off a bit, but not appreciably.

The one way that the Chinese citizens did show their unhappiness with the situation was for them to throw their empty glass coffee cups out of the open windows and on to the tracks as they finished their drink. After a while the Americans got the idea of throwing the cups out of the open windows also. It some how gave one satisfaction to hear the glass shattering on the ground.

As we discussed the heat with May Wah, our Chinese American guide, she told us of the reputation of the three cities we were in the process of visiting. Shanghai, Hangchow and Nanjing were called the "three ovens" by the Chinese. Of course, in the American brochures, there was no reference to that.

We arrived in Nanjing and visited this ancient capitol for a day or two and then flew on to Beijing and the cooler north.

On our second trip to China six years later, we did not take the train ride into the three ovens even though it was in a much more comfortable time of the year. But we did take a train ride from Beijing to Cheng de in the extreme north almost to the Mongolian border. There was no airport in Cheng de and the only reasonable way to get there was by train. This train ride was so much more comfortable. Boachan, a wonderful tour guide, told us if we could not make it to Tibet to see the ancient Tibetan monastery we should at least go to Cheng de, to see the palaces north of the Great Wall. They were built about six hundred years ago during the Ming dynasty and were absolutely magnificent. As usual he was right—these were awesome. The one problem is Cheng de is not well known, and does not even have an airport. The population is slightly over two hundred thousand and they do not get many tourists. As a matter of fact we never met anyone who had been there.

The six of us making the trip, Phyllis, Tom, Baochen, Heather, Lila and I boarded the train from the Beijing station and in a few minutes we were out of the capitol and into the countryside. The train twisted and turned through a magnificent uphill ride to and though the mountains of northern China. In about an hour, we reached the Great Wall and this time saw it from a very different perspective. I stood on the platform between two cars and watched the train meander through the mountainside. There were little villages everywhere as there are all over China. Every time there was the slightest piece of flat land there would be a little cottage or village. As the train curved around the mountains I was able to see the front and back cars turning through and around the mountains. I imagined how the Mongols hundreds of years before streamed through these mountain on their way to attack the Chinese to the south.

Then at last we reached flat terrain and we saw mile after mile of rice fields. It was magnificent. Each little farm had its farmer, and his wife, and child planting little stalks of rice. All of a sudden, Heather broke out her tape recorder and started to play music. The sound of music somehow enticed Baochan to get up and dance. His rhythm was so catching that Lila, in an instant got up and joined him. Then before we knew it, Heather and I also joined in the festivities. The only ones who did not join the fun were Tom and Phyllis. Tom was having some physical problems and just wanted to sleep them off.

Before long we arrived at the Cheng de train station and we had the next three days to enjoy the wonderful summer palaces of the Emperors. It was a beautiful area of China and I certainly would not have missed it. Each day we walked through another palace or strolled along a lake and we came back with some of the most spectacular pictures of our entire trip.

When it was time to return to Beijing, we reluctantly boarded our train back through the mountains and over the Great Wall and a few more days in exciting Beijing.

As I think back to our two "training" experiences, they were so very different. From the heat of summer to the wonder of the mountainous northern country in the late autumn they were certainly something to write home about.

Imperial Park Cheng de, China,

Imperial Bridge, Cheng de, China,

2. The Yangtze River Sunrise

The alarm clock sounded and with the first ring I was out of bed diving for my dungarees and T-shirt. It was six o'clock on this October morning and I noiselessly left our stateroom. It was our third day on the Yangtze River and the beginning of the highlight of our boat trip.

This was the morning when the Yangtze Princess would make its way through the Three Gorges—narrow sections of the river where its steep vertical sides are less than one hundred feet apart and our ship must maneuver carefully between the magnificent five-hundred-foot-high mountain walls. I was quite familiar with it since Lila and I had gone down the Yangtze River eight years before. During that trip we also saw a wonderful sunrise and I was determined to see it once again. I knew this would be my last time because the Chinese government was building a dam and associated lake system called the Yangtze River Project, (the world's largest) which was going to flood almost half of the gorges. To one million Chinese people and me this was an absolute shame but to 50 million others it meant electricity.

What is so special about the 'Gorges' sunrise is when you are there at just the right time you experience as many as five sunrises in a single morning! How is that possible you ask? Between the turning of the river and the location of the mountains, and at just the right time of year, the sun rises, then sets, and almost immediately repeats the process again and again. It is an exciting vision especially for one who loves sunrises, and I am one of those sunrise lovers.

There I was, creeping along the gangway on route to the ship's bow hoping to see that wonderful sunrise again. It was a perfect day. The air was crisp and damp. The clouds were in there appointed places, beautifully interspersed among the mountains, as I arrived at the bow of our cruise ship. I was the first to arrive so I had a wonderful grandstand view of the oncoming scene. The light rays were just beginning to sneak through the clouds and the sky took on its rainbow of yellows, reds and pinks. Then all of a sudden the bright beginning of the incredibly red ball of fire began peeking up over the tops of the mountains and through the clouds. The streaks of color were everywhere—between the clouds and along the mountain rim; it was a magnificent scene.

But then as if by magic, as our ship continued to steam, the mountains blocked the sun and made it appear as if it were setting again. The sky darkened and before I knew it, the sun was down and the sky grew grayish black and it was night once more. Then in a while, the magic of the sunlight repeated itself, and for the second time I had the wonderful sunrise experience over again. The sun rose to begin its self appointed rounds and the beauty of the sunrise presented me with its morning treat and the red ball of brilliance blasted through the brightened sky. The colors showered down upon me. Then the magical process repeated itself with a magnificent sunset. I thought to myself, just how much of this beauty can one take in a single morning? But there it was, with the sun once again coming, though meekly this time, but nevertheless the rays of sunlight gave me a third treat. Then the magic of the heavens and the turning of the Princess caused the sun to set. What beauty hast those heavens above!

I knew that this treasure would not last forever and that eventually the sun's rays would overcome the height of the mountaintops. But again we experienced yet another sunrise and sunset as the Yangtze Princess continued its journey through the gorges. We had now gone though four sunrises and as many sunsets. Would the treat never end? But, finally for the fifth and final time, the most powerful rays of the sun came to light up the day! Through the clouds and over the mountains, and down the glistening river waters, it shined directly toward our ship. In one most powerful rush, at last, the sun made its ultimate entry brightening this October day. Overcoming all, the sun had risen.

Chinese Family crossing the Yangtzi River, Wuhan, China,

Lila in a Carrying Chair along the Yangtzi

Squeezing through a narrow gorge on the Yangtzi,

3. A Pair of Swinging Bridges

In the valley of Yosemite Park, Joe and I once took a nice short walk across a very peaceful bridge over the Mercer River called "The Swinging Bridge." The Yosemite bridge reminded me of a real swinging bridge deep in the heart of Southwest China just outside of Cheng du—the latter, however, was very different. Whereas the Yosemite Bridge was stable and gave one a sense of security, the

Chinese Swinging Bridge did just what the name describes—swinging and made one feel very unstable!

The Chinese bridge is about six feet wide and does not allow vehicles. The pedestrians like to test it out by swinging it from side to side. It sways violently as you try to hold your balance. In the 1990s I was in good physical condition, yet I needed to use all my physical strength to remain stable. While I stood on the bridge a few young and wild local teenagers caused the bridge to swing over two feet in either direction. Naturally, the teens found it exciting to make the bridge move, but from the perspective of an adult, it was frightening, so I held on for dear life.

The bridge extends the length of almost 800 feet across the Min River and was originally part of a huge irrigation project that was the first and largest irrigation system ever built in China. The Min River, a tributary of the Yangtze River, tended to flood wildly every few years and destroy entire fields of rice crops. Therefore, a team of Chinese engineers headed by a brilliant civil engineer named Li Bing designed a "moving island" that would allow the river waters to flow into the fields in a controlled manner, instead of flooding the Yangtze River. This was an incredibly ingenious design and the system, built in 256 B. C., is still in operation (one of the oldest continuing engineering feats in existence). The Swinging Bridge was built as part of the project to reach the "moving island" and was designed so well that the original bridge lasted until the eighteenth century when it finally came down in a storm.

A replica of Li Bing's original design for the Swinging Bridge was built in 1974. It is said that it even swings similarly to the original bridge. Let's hope that this one will last two thousand years like the first one built by good old Li Bing, unless too many teenagers "test" it out.

Lila crossing the Swinging Bridge, Leshon, China

4. Terra Cotta Figures Come to Life

Thirty years ago in the spring of 1974, a young Chinese farmer in the outskirts of the ancient city of Sian made a rather startling discovery, although he did not know it at the time. As he was plowing his fields, his plow went somewhat deeper than normal and it hit an unusual object. It was a piece of man-made terra cotta (processed clay) that apparently had some painting on it. Wisely, as time would tell, he took the piece into the museum in Sian and showed it to one of the archeologists there.

They went out to the farmer's field and began looking for more samples and in a matter of just a few hours they found many more pieces and the discovery of a lifetime was about to reveal itself.

The farmer and the archeologist began to dig through the field and went down for a foot or two and found a few more clay pieces. Then for the next several days they decided to go down to a depth of six feet to determine once and for all what these pieces of clay really were. Sure enough at the depth of about six feet the archeologist came upon another piece of clay that looked something like a face and it was just too large to be a toy. Now for certain, they knew there were more pieces to discover. Within a week more and more pieces were being picked up as they dug deeper and deeper. A report was put out to Beizing and several more experts joined the pair.

Before long experts from all over the country would be coming out to look at this incredible find. Within a year almost one thousand life-size figures, or significant parts of them, had been discovered all over the farmer's now famous field. Research regarding the area now determined that the pieces of terra cotta were part of an army of figures constructed over two thousand years ago by the artisans of the first Chinese Emperor, Qin.

The size and extent of the find grew larger and shortly thereafter, an area approximately twice the size of a football field was enclosed to protect this invaluable find. Archeologists from all over the world were flocking to see this sight, then being called the eighth wonder of the world.

Within the first ten years much research was done about this Emperor. He assumed the throne when he was thirteen years old. He was less than eighteen years old when his astounding commanding abilities were made known throughout the land. Over the next thirty years he ruled and unified China as no other man ever did. Before Qin's time China was divided into many small provinces that often fought among each other. But Emperor Qin unified the country with his power and dominance. Shortly after he crowned himself Emperor, he began to consider his immortality and began the project that rivals the Egyptian Pyramids in its immensity.

Within four years, a fully detailed article had been written for National Geographic Magazine that described this historic find. The story told about this emperor describes his desire for immortality and his building an army of terra cotta figures to protect him against his enemies in the after-life.

Being an avid National Geographic reader, I read the story with great interest. Although I had always dreamed of going to mainland China, now I was sure. I was determined that within the next five years I would visit these magnificent figures. But it was ten years before Lila and I finally signed up with a Lindblad tour of thirty to visit this land of mystery and excitement. By the time we had arrived thousands of tourists had came from all over the world to view this unbelievable army of Terra Cotta figures. Some of the pieces that were found are in very poor condition. Currently, in some areas very little has been done waiting for new and sophisticated equipment to be developed to protect the items being located.

As the years went by, the excavation sight was extended even further and chariots and hundreds of horses were found throughout the area. Even an entire army headquarters was discovered in the 1990's. In this area of Sian over the next ten years many more figures probably will continue to be found. This was the kind of discovery that tickles the imagination and encourages the determination to visit this wondrous place.

The historical data now shows that these figures were built around 200 B. C. As the first real ruler of this huge land, Emperor Qin could be considered the Alexander the Great of China.

During our first visit to China in 1989, Lila and I stood on the platform overlooking the army of figures about fifteen feet below our viewing level. Even from this height the figures looked large and life-size. There were over twenty compartments stretching the length of about two football fields. There were already over seven thousand figures that extended as far as the eye could see. In one corner several workers were putting together broken pieces of clay into additional soldiers of the emperor's army. I watched to see them put together an archeologist's, "jigsaw puzzle".

In our second trip to China six years later, another one thousand figures including the army headquarters had been dug up. Now that the figures were enclosed in a more permanent building, the rules about photographing the figures were more strictly enforced. As is usually the case one tourist took some pictures despite the signs saying "No Photographs" written in English all around the building.

As I looked down at the scene, I imagined Emperor Qin reviewing this army of lifeless troops. Each of these elite guards was individual and distinct from the other. Since each one of these seven thousand figures had different facial expressions as well as uniforms, one could only assume models were used by the artisans to carve them.

Standing there and gazing at all of this, I began to imagine myself commanding the seven thousand guards and presenting them to the Emperor. I could see myself sweeping down the row upon row of soldiers looking at each one to see that he was properly dressed and in correct uniform. All the soldiers stood at attention for the hour it took to complete the inspection. It was so exciting to think of an army of thousands standing at attention in honor of one of the most important men of all time. The Emperor and I were also in our full uniform. We looked splendid! It was such fun to imagine being in charge of this whole army and presenting them to the emperor. I was his senior advisor and he looked to me for council and advice. Even though he was the Emperor, he looked to me for my experience and it felt great to be in the position of giving advice to an emperor. Then Lila touched me and my daydream vanished.

Historically, when Emperors died, the live family members and guards were actually buried with him. In the city of Nanjing we viewed an ancient museum that was the burying place of a ruler. Lila and I were shocked to hear that the family members and guards were buried with him. Today that tradition no longer exists. One may think that Emperor Qin was good to his troops by building the terra-cotta figures instead of burying a whole army of real people with him.

Six years later we again visited Sian and its terra-cotta figures. Although much progress had been made between our two visits of 1989 and 1995, I am expecting that even more will be excavated during the next decade. The highlight of course, will be the excavation of the emperor and the empress's tombs themselves. On our latest visit we saw two chariots were excavated. I can imagine how the emperor rode the streets of Sian with the thousands of citizens cheering him on. Although the chariots that were excavated were found crushed and almost totally destroyed, with much work and effort, they have been reconstructed and once again look as they did before they were buried, two millenniums ago.

As had happened before, I began to daydream as I gazed at the chariots. I imagined being in the first chariot, with Emperor Qin in the one behind me. We each had a driver controlling the four horses that majestically pulling the chariots and we were having a race. What an exciting period that must have been!

Lila and I with our friends, Phyllis and Tom, and our guide Heather walked through the corridors of the exhibition hall with its amazing collection of soldiers, horses and chariots. As we left the exhibition hall, there was a small size but very accurately designed chariot on sale in the little souvenir shop. It was an almost exact replica of Emperor Qin's completely enclosed chariot designed to protect him against any disgruntled citizens who may attack him as he passed through the streets of Sian.

I was intrigued with the chariot and I wanted to have one. Lila and I huddled together and decided to buy the one that was the exact replica of the Emperor's chariot. Although, I liked the terra-cotta soldiers, Lila was more impressed with the chariot. Of course the cost of the chariot was expensive and even if the cost of shipping it back to New York City was high, it was one of those once-in-a-lifetime purchases and we went for it. To this day it rests majestically in our Manhattan apartment in a chamber especially designed for it, where it is a conversation piece, par excellence.

6. Leshan's Giant Buddha

In the center of China in the Province of Sichuan is the city of Chongqing with its ten million people. The four of us, Phyllis, Tom, Lila and I, drove in a station wagon from there southwest to the ancient city of Leshan about one-hundred miles.

Phyllis and Lila were old friends from Long Island, New York school district, and both of them retired at the same time shortly before our 1995 trip to China. They were enjoying their time together. Although Lila and I had been to China six years before, that trip did not include a view of the Leshan Buddha. But this time I knew this was one highlight we were not going to miss.

Leshan, a city of about two million people is where three rivers meet in the heart of the rice belt. One of the most significant memories, which every tourist has of Leshan, is its huge three hundred foot high Buddha cut into the center of the mountain on the opposite side of the river from the center of the city. Thousands of visitors leave from the city port to view the Giant Buddha from sea or land.

Our trip included seeing Buddha from both sides—from the land walking down to the river edge, and from the boat traveling in the river. In the morning we drove through the city and up to mountain ridge. There with hundreds of other tourists we walked up to the face of the Buddha and right to his ear which is six feet tall. It was an incredible feeling. Then I walked down along one side all the way to his toenail. As I descended this treacherous narrow stairway barely wide enough for one person, I had to stop every few flights to make way for the other people coming up from the bottom. There were thirty flights of stairs from the toes to the head and it took quite an effort to descent to the sea level where hundreds of people stood around waiting to take pictures sitting on the Buddha's toes. But in those days, I was strong and determined and never let something as daunting as three hundred steps stop me from seeing a unique vision like the toes of the Leshan Buddha.

The rest of my group stayed at the top but I hiked to the bottom of Buddha toes. After a while I reached the lowest floor at the sea level of the mountain. In front of me I could see the sight-seeing boats out in the harbor bobbing up and down while other vessels waited their turn off shore. Their guides talked to them all about the Buddha by means of an amplifier.. I could hear Chinese being spoken to the fifty or so people on these ferries, one of which we would be taking that afternoon. But for the moment I was happy to be waiting my turn to stand upon one of Buddha's toenails and have someone take my picture. Can you just imagine a toenail big enough to hold four little Chinese tourists and me?

After spending fifteen or twenty minutes at the feet of the Buddha, I started the ascent up to the Buddha's headdress, the entire three hundred feet. It was an invigorating climb to say the least, but I made it and met the others at the top.

In the afternoon we drove to the port and waited for over an hour for a ferry to take us out to the statue. There was a long line of tourists because that day there was a special group of tourists taking the trip to see the Buddha. There were over three hundred mayors from all over China attending a meeting in Leshan and after their meeting they were taken on the trip out to see the mountain-carved Buddha. They all went on different boats.

At long last we got on a boat with an English-speaking guide and went out to see Buddha from the angle of the river. Although the water was somewhat rough, we did not capsize and had a magnificent view of Buddha at the water level. As I saw those mayors from all over China standing in their boats, I wondered what their prayers to Buddha were all about that day.

Here is a story that our guide told us on our afternoon boat ride to the Giant Buddha:

In about the Eighth Century A. D., long before Marco Polo visited China, the confluence three rivers, Dadu, Min and Qingyi, at the city of Leshan caused the boats coming down the northern most river to often capsize, especially during the heavy rainy season, one or two boats overturned daily. There was also a great loss of life when these boats would sink. The city fathers sat at a meeting one day and decided that the only thing that would stop the loss of life and destruction of these boats, was to build a Giant Buddha in the face of the mountain to command that the rivers no longer be violent. So, many thousands of Chinese started to work on the project. They cut into the mountain and erected this huge three hundred foot Buddha. In the course of building the Giant Buddha, the rock and dirt from the mountain side were thrown into the river. At last, after almost one hundred years, the Buddha was completed and this huge structure built into the Leshan mountains was a reality. It was a magnificent carving several times the height of the figures of the presidents in Mt. Rushmore.

Well, lo and behold, the waters of the Leshan rivers did actually slow down. The realistic theory behind the variation in tidal changes and the resultant changes in tidal speed was that the dirt and stone thrown from the mountainside filled up one of the rivers and causing the whirlpools to diminish. So the ships stopped sinking and the sailors stopped drowning. Of course, the local citizens gave credit to Buddha for his magnificent wonders. During the next millennium, thousands of visitors came to Leshan to pray for more miracles from Buddha. First came visitors from the Province of Sichuan, then from all over China, and now the world.

6. Sociology: 102

A couple of years ago in my first travel book called "The Chinese Walking Stick", I told the sad but true story (Sociology 101) of a little girl we saw dying on the streets of Fengie. As we saw this dying girl and were told to keep quiet about it, I knew it had to do with a big problem throughout all of China. Now it is coming to that country's forefront and the world is realizing this sad tragedy.

China is a vast nation and now has the world's fastest-growing economy. It is confronting a self-perpetuated demographic disaster that some experts describe as "genecide"—the phenomenom caused by millions of families resorting to abortion and infanticide to make sure their one child that is allowed per family, is a boy.

The age-old bias for boys, combined with China's draconian one-child policy imposed since 1980, has produced what Gu Baochang, a leading Chinese expert on family planning, described as "the largest, the highest, and the longest" gender imbalance in the world.

Ancient practice

For centuries, Chinese families without sons feared poverty and neglect. The male offspring represented continuity of lineage and protection in old age. The traditional thinking is best described in the ancient "Book of Songs" (700 B.C.):
"When a son is born,
Let him sleep on the bed,
Clothe him with fine clothes,
And give him jade to play...
When a daughter is born,
Let her sleep on the ground,
Wrap her in common wrappings,
And give broken tiles to play..."

After the Communists took power in 1949, Mao Zedong rejected traditional Malthusian arguments that population growth would eventually outrun food supply, and firmly regarded China's huge population (then with an annual birth rate of 3.7 percent) an asset. It proved not to be. Without a state-mandated birth control program, China's sex ratio in the 1960's and 70's remained normal. Then in the early '80s, China began enforcing an ambitious demographic engineering policy to limit families to one-child, as part of its strategy to fast-track economic modernization. The policy resulted in a slashed annual birth rate of 1.29 percent by 2002, or the prevention of some 300 million births, and the current population of close to 1.3 billion.

Missing girls

From a relatively normal ratio of 108.5 boys to 100 girls in the early 1980s, the male surplus progressively rose to 111 in 1990, 116 in 2000, and is now is close to 120 boys for each 100 girls, according to a Chinese think-tank report.

The shortage of women is creating a "huge societal issue," recently warned U.N. resident coordinator Khalid Malik.
Along with HIV/AIDS and environmental degradation, he said this was one of the three biggest challenges facing China.

"In eight to ten years, they lack something like 40 to 60 million women," he said, adding that it will have "enormous implications for China's prostitution industry and human trafficking."

China's own population experts have been warning for years about the looming gender crisis.

"The loss of female births due to illegal prenatal sex determination and sex-selective abortions and female infanticide will affect the true sex ratio at birth and at young ages, creating an unbalanced population sex structure in the future and resulting in potentially serious social problems," argued Peking University's chief demographer back in 1993.

Prenatal sex selection

The abortion of female fetuses and infanticide was aided by the spread of cheap and portable ultra-sound scanners in the 1980's. Illegal mobile scanning and back street hospitals provide a sex scan for as little as $50, according to one report.

"Prenatal sex selection was probably the primary cause, if not the sole cause, for the continuous rise of the sex ratio at birth," said population expert Prof. Chu Junhong in another report. A slew of other reports have confirmed this disturbing demographic trend.

In a 2002 survey conducted in a central China village, more than 300 of the 820 women had abortions and more than a third of them admitted they were trying to select their baby's sex. According to a report by the International Planned Parenthood Federation, the vast majority of aborted fetuses, more than 70 percent, were female, citing the abortion of up to 750,000 female fetuses in China in 1999.

A report by Zhang Qing, population researcher of the Chinese Academy of Social Sciences, said the gender imbalance is "statistically related to the high death rate of female babies, with female death rate at age zero in the city or rural areas consistently higher than male baby death rate." Only seven of China's 29 provinces are within the world's average sex ratio. Zhang Qing's report cited eight "disaster provinces" from North to South China, where there were 26 to 38 percent more boys than girls. In the last census in 2000, there were nearly 19 million more boys than girls in the 0-15 age group.

"We have to act now or the problem will become very serious," said Peking University sociologist Prof. Xia Xueluan. He cited the need to strengthen social welfare system in the countryside to weaken the traditional preference for boys.

Gravity of imbalance was beginning to be felt. The hint of "serious" problems ahead can be seen in the increasing cases of human trafficking as bachelors try to "purchase" their wives. China's police have freed more than 42,000 kidnapped women and children from 2001 to 2003.

The vast army of surplus males could pose a threat to China's stability, argued two Western scholars. Valerie M. Hudson and Andrea M. Den Boer, who recently wrote a book on the "Security Implications of Asia's Surplus Male Population," cited two rebellions in disproportionately male areas in Manchu Dynasty. The question is what kind of a society will exist with an unbalance of 40 million males? Will there be a mass flooding of these males throughout the world? The age-old question will arise, "When China sneezes, will the whole world get a cold?"

TAIWAN

7. Taiwan To Suit

During my many years visiting Taiwan, I was often attracted to the "made-to-measure" clothing industry flourishing all over Taipei. Throughout the old sections of the city there were little stalls where one could buy a suit at a reasonable price. In one area alone I counted over one hundred tiny shops all advertising some version of "Hand Made Suits to Order." During one of my trips I took the plunge and went for a hand-made suit. It was an interesting experience.

I arrived in Taipei late one Sunday evening after the usual thirteen-hour trip to Narita, Japan, the three-hour wait at the Tokyo airport and finally the three-hour flight to Taipei. After the long trip I went to sleep almost immediately. On Monday I met with our business rep to plan out the week's schedule. I usually stayed for a week leaving for New York some time on Friday afternoon.

I never had much of a problem with 'jet lag', and by Monday evening I was ready for a dinner with Jim Adams, Vice President of Marketing, and several of the Taiwanese Air Force personnel. Before dinner I walked around the hustling and bustling downtown Taipei. We usually stayed at the Hilton, which was just across the boulevard from the National Railway Station. It was one of the busiest sections of the city with buses coming and going from all parts of the north. The streets were crowded with thousands of bicyclists and motorbikes, often each one was loaded with an entire family. Many times I saw motorbikes with a husband, wife and as many as three kids all jammed on the two-wheeler. Scores of these little vehicles would be jammed on the roads, weaving in and out of traffic in a most precarious manner. It amazed me how they would drive right up to and against the buses and trucks and miraculously avoid an accident. But the Chinese are extremely dexterous people and, as if by magic, just miss those huge monster buses without getting wiped out. I walked the four blocks from the Hilton watching the scenes of near mass-destruction at each corner.

At last I reached the street crowded with a hundred or more of those made-to-order tailoring shops, each little stall had dozens of bolts of woolen material all labeled, "Made In Scotland." which I doubted. I walked through the area in complete disbelief, that there could possibly be so many little tailoring shops in the entire world. The owners or their sons or brothers would stand out in front inviting you to come in and buy a "tailor-made suit," with the usual "be ready tomorrow," "best tailoring in Taiwan" or some such verbal advertisement. That was just about all the English they knew.

I do not know to this day but somehow or other I picked one out of the hundred and walked in. I was immediately inundated with bolts of woolens and worsteds as the owner would drape the material over my shoulder. I heard, "You like this?" or "Make up beautiful suit for you with this material", "I make suit for you by tomorrow." After looking at the dozens of materials, I finally chose one that the tailor said was the best and most expensive material in the shop. It was a navy blue with a white thin strip. We bargained for a while and at last, agreed on a price of one hundred dollars. Then he pulled out a book of styles and I had to make dozens of decisions in the span of a few minutes regarding my new suit.

I never knew there were so many decisions that must be made—double breasted, single breasted, two button, three button, three-inch lapel, two-inch lapel, two or three-button cuff, on and on went the routine. On all the previous occasions when I have bought suits at Bonds or Ripleys in Manhattan, I just looked at the completed product and said yes or no to what I liked. It was that simple. Now getting a suit had become a major undertaking. I didn't mind after awhile—it made me feel important.

I stayed in the shop for over one half-hour until all the measurements and designs were complete. My little tailor then asked me where I was staying, to which I answered the Hilton.

He said that he would be there tomorrow night at seven. I thought it was great that he would actually be there the next night with my suit. Since that would be Tuesday and I was not leaving until Friday. I felt assured there would be no problem. Tuesday evening at seven before I was going to dinner with my rep, the little tailor knocked at the hotel room door with my suit, or so I thought. He and his assistant walked in and opened the package that just shocked me. There must have been a half dozen pieces of my material but they where not sewn together. He busily laid all the jacket pieces over me and started pinning everything together. When I said I thought the suit would be all made, he said it would be a better fit if he measured it over me again. I rushed him out because of my dinner date. He said he would have the suit on Wednesday night at seven.

"Ok," I said, "Be sure you are done."

On Wednesday evening he again showed up at seven and this time he had a finished suit. I put it on and looked at myself in the mirror. I liked the material and the design but the jacket did not fit as well as I thought it would considering all his efforts. The shoulders seemed to overhang. He said he would fix them. Time was getting short but the tailor told me not to worry that he would have the finished suit by Thursday night.

What I had expected to be a one-day effort like they advertised turned into a multi-day event. It was now getting close to the time I was scheduled to leave for New York. If he missed Thursday night I could actually be flying back without my new suit. But then again I realized I had not paid for it so I had little to be concerned about.

But Thursday evening as I was going out for dinner in came my two Taiwanese friends, all smiles.

"Here is your suit," they proclaimed as they opened up the package.

Yes! There it was. Finished beautifully and as I tried it on, it did fit to perfection. Every seam was matched. My tailor showed me how the white stripes at the shoulder fit perfectly to the body of the jacket, how the back stripes were laid in so they touched each other and the pants stripes too were in perfect alignment, These touches of class, I had never noticed in a suit before. I had never seen any of these features in my Bond suits. I was now conscious of and feeling great about them. That night I strode out of my room wearing my made-to-perfection suit, and at dinner, I was careful not to get a stain on it.

Buddist Ceremony, Taipei, Taiwan

9. The GI Party At The Grand

In the beginning there were chop sticks and chow mein. It was not ten years since General Chang Kai Chek left the main land just one step ahead of Mao. Slowly the agrarian society of Taiwan began developing into a capitalistic business class. The thousands of intellectuals from the mainland became the business people of the island of Taiwan. Communism lay on the other side of the China Sea but it could have been ten thousand miles away for all the interest it was drawing on the island. The students of the families of Taiwan were aggressively learning English and applied for graduate schools all over the United States. The late 1950s was an exciting time with great opportunity for growth on the island and a tremendous surge of interest in education and democracy. Those not interested in either of those subjects became interested in technology.

Meanwhile ten thousand miles away on Madison Avenue and Sixty-First Street, the General Instrument CEO, Moses Shapiro, was trying to make a go of the new technology called Semiconductors. The diodes and transistors being developed in the laboratories in Jamaica, New York started to be produced in Woonsocket, Rhode Island. But the costs of labor in Rhode Island became prohibitively high and we were losing ten cents with each device.

In the summer of 1957, Monty took a business/pleasure trip to Taiwan to learn about other companies opening semiconductor factories outside of the capitol of Taiwan. He came back excited and convinced that Taipei was an ideal place to open such a factory. The labor cost was in the range of twenty-five cents an hour and it was primarily that factor, which convinced him to open a plant there. The factory cost in Rhode Island was more than ten times that of Taiwan and it did not take him a minute to see that doing production in Taipei made economic sense.

The first time I heard of the Taiwan facility, it came with a parable—the Taipei production workers, when they started, did not know which end of the soldering iron to grab. But, in less than a year, diodes and transistors started to come off the production line. In less than two years, the Woonsocket plant was phased out despite previous labor promises.

Over the years that I visited the Taipei plant, it grew from hundreds to thousands of workers. The first time was in the 1970's when I remember driving past horses and carts taking the people to work. The taxi which drove me to the plant that day had to stop a few times to make way for chickens and goats crossing the roads. But each time I visited the plant the progress seemed more and more spectacular. On my second visit to the plant, I met a tall handsome American who dressed beautifully which I presumed was Taiwanese made-to-order suits. He proudly gave me a tour of the factory. He introduced himself as Jim Klein. During my many trip I met Jim often and on one of my trips he introduced me to a beautiful Chinese lady named Helen who had joined the GI personal staff. It was clear that she was well cultured. On the next trip Jim announced that he and Helen had married. To me, they became the glue that kept the General Instrument family together.

During the middle 1980's I often made trips to the island to sell Radar Warning Receivers to the Taiwan Air Force. On one occasion my visit coincided with

General Instrument's celebration to commemorate it's twenty-fifth anniversary. It shocked me to think that one quarter of a century had passed since our first little factory opened at the outskirts of Taipei. During the middle eighties, Moses Shapiro, who built General Instrument into a multi-divisional, billion-dollar company during the two previous decades, passed away and Frank Hickey became its chief.

Both Frank Hickey, CEO. and George Safiol, Corporate President had become devoted to the success of the Taiwan operations and they decided to make the 25th anniversary a fabulous celebration. Because I happened to be in Taiwan at the time, Jim Klein, then President of GI Taiwan invited me to the affair. It was a celebration that was not outdone by any previous or subsequent party in the company's history.

Any affair held in the nations capitol would naturally be at The Grand Hotel. The Hotel sits astride the Hill. One sees it for several miles in all direction with its Chinese Red Pagoda shape and the magnificent bright lights that announce you are approaching Madame Chang's masterpiece. What the White House is to Washington, the Grand hotel is to Taiwan. Madame Chang Kai Check supervised the design of the hotel in the 1950's shortly after the country became a republic. One walks through the twenty-foot high doors into a magnificent marble lobby with world famous paintings and sculptures. It is breathtaking to go through the hotel's convention rooms and dining halls that compare to the world famous hotels of New York and London.

Jim Klein arranged the party and invited the most prestigious and famous names in the land including the Premier Sun, to the General Instrument 25th Anniversary.

The cocktail part attended by well over one thousand guests preceded the dinner. Frank Hickey and George Safiol spoke at the dinner and thanked all the key G.I. employees who were so instrumental in making the Taipei plant such a success.

The next day an Olympics Extravaganza was arranged for the entire twenty-five thousand people who currently or previously worked at the GI facilities in the area. A stadium was rented where hundreds of activities were held. The highlight of the day was the drawing of prizes with a Honda automobile as the first prize awarded. The winning number was drawn and after several minutes no one responded. Since the winner must be in the stadium according to the rules, a second number was drawn. As the holder of the second ticket leaped up to declare his prize, the holder of the first winning ticket walked back into the stadium from the restroom. He too claimed the prize. After much discussion, the General

Instrument executives decided that the most diplomatic solution was to give each winner a car. It was a weekend that GI executives and employees will never forget.

10. Dinner For Two In Osaka

My Japanese rep, Tom Takano, and I had visited a potential subcontractor, Mitzubishi Electric, during one of my trips to Japan in conjunction with our P-3C program. As part of the contract from JDA, the Japanese Defense Agency insisted we do a specific amount of our system in Japan. We planned to use Mitzubishi as our subcontractor, but before we gave them the subcontract I wanted to see whether or not they had the capability to make Radar Warning Receivers. I spent an entire day reviewing their factory and they gave me full tour of their plant. It was extremely thorough and detailed, taking the entire day. By the time we were finished it was so late in the afternoon, I decided we should spend the night in Osaka. It is a big modern city with nice hotels and restaurants.

After registering at a downtown hotel, my rep suggested that we visit a seafood place that he said was one of the best in Osaka. I imagined the restaurant would be similar to American seafood restaurant and I said, "Of course". It was a block or two from the hotel so we walked to it. As we arrived I noticed it was jammed with Orientals and I was the only Occidental in the place. The restaurant did not have tables but rather had only counter places. We waited for a few minutes and finally got two seats in the center. As I sat down, I got the experience of my life. Right in front of me was a large pond with a series of boards straddling it. Standing on one of the boards was a man wearing hip boots and in his hands was a long pole with a net attached. I watched as he used the net to scoop up one of the fish swimming in the pond. As he caught the fish, he flung it at one of the counters where another man took the fish in his hand and sliced it up with the knife held in the other hand. In an instant he put it on a plate and served it to a waiting customer. I watched the process several times and realized that the customers were getting their fish in the freshest possible way. The fish were actually still wiggling when the pieces were served.

My friend watched my expression and said, "You have not been to a Japanese seafood restaurant before, have you?"

"No," I admitted. Do they serve anything else here?" I asked.

He suggested I get shrimp. "OK" I said, thinking that the shrimp would be cooked as we get them in the United States. "That would be fine."

My rep ordered one of the fish that was caught and sliced up right in front of us. I watched as he swallowed his wiggling fish. With his chopsticks he put the pieces of the white fish in his mouth and chewed on them with vigor. I could see he was enjoying himself, but was glad I had not ordered it. Then my shrimp came. To my shock they were not cooked at all, but were raw shrimp in the gray-ish color that I had seen in fish stores, not the red cooked shrimp that was in shrimp cocktails. I tried to eat one and almost gagged. I could see that dinner that night was going to be an ordeal. I sat there looking at the shrimp and trying to figure out how I was going to get through dinner that evening. I played with my shrimp for while and finally admitted to my rep that this was not what I had in mind either. By this time my companion was almost done with his dinner.

He suggested that we go back to the hotel's restaurant to which I hardly agreed. At the hotel I had a delicious steak and he enjoyed watching me eat it, but he probably was content with his fish dinner.

4

COLUMBUS' DISCOVERIES

1. The Caribbean: Then and Now—

Lila and I began our initial Caribbean vacation in 1985 to the island of Barbados, a few hundred miles from where Columbus made his first landfall in what is now the Dominican Republic. In the 15th century Columbus and his three ships, The Nina, The Pinta and The Santa Maria, landed in the heart of the very busy area called the Caribbean. Many native tribes were actively growing vegetables and other life sustaining foods for hundreds of years prior to Columbus's landing.

Over the next ten years Columbus traveled back and forth three times from Spain to Central America. One might say that Columbus was the first regular tourist to the Caribbean Islands. Of course, the word "America" did not come into existence until the middle of the 16th century when a Dutch map maker was the first to print this word on a world map. Amerigo Vespucci named South America, which later extended the northern hemisphere.

Interestingly, Amerigo traveled further than Columbus by going from Portugal to the southern hemisphere.

For the next five hundred years the Caribbean probably changed less than most other areas of the North America. It is still a tropical wonderland with many forested areas that may not be too different from when Columbus arrived.

Our first cruise into the Caribbean was in a sailing vessel, like Columbus I thought. We boarded the Windstar from the port of Bridgetown, Barbados. The Windstar is a four-mast magnificent sailing ship with all the luxury and comfort that Columbus and his men could never have known. One might say that the only similarity between Columbus' ships and The Windstar is that they were all powered by wind.

The Windstar is a glamorous four-mast computer-based sailing vessel built in the late 1980s. It has over 22,000 square feet of sail, which is more than the three Columbus ships combined. Columbus' ships each had fifty men to furl and unfurl the sails; The Windstar had just three. There are scores of luxury ships cruising the Caribbean Sea, but The Windstar is very different than the others. This cruise ship is four hundred feet long with only 125 staterooms. It is not a crowded multi-storied, ten elevator type of cruise ship. Its capacity is less than ten percent of the tourists on board most of the huge ships. This small ship gives one the privilege of an escape to the islands without bumping into hoards of people.

Our Windstar cruise gave us the opportunity to spend seven exciting days visiting five wonderful islands. After leaving Barbados, we sailed to Tobago Bay, St. Vincent, Grenada, Martinique and St. Lucia; these are also known as The Windward Islands. Each island has its own distinct characteristics. Upon docking at each port we were offered a well-organized group tour usually on a bus or a series of buses. However, we often found freelance English-speaking individual guides available at the ports. This was our preferred way of touring an island because we would see exciting places around each island at our own pace. Touring with an individual tour guide was more fun and usually at a lower cost than the excursions arranged by the cruise ship.

Every once in a while we would meet another couple that shared our idea about taking private tours. When we did find such a couple who was compatible with us, it was even more fun. On our trip along the Windward Islands, we met such a couple, The McGraths, from New England. During this entire trip they often traveled with us, and we enjoyed our times together. For years afterward we remained friends with them on an annual Christmas card basis.

Each day was a different experience and a new adventure. One day we climbed a palm tree to pick a coconut, and videotaped ourselves slurping its milk. The pictures showing us with coconut liquid dripping all over our faces are unforgettable. One day our guide gave us a lecture on how a cocoa bean is processed. On another day we spent an exciting time listening to Calypso music and watching a steel drum band. On another day, we spent the afternoon snorkeling off the coast of Tobago Bay, where every time we came up for air, the locals would try to sell us tie-dyed tee shirts hanging from a clothesline.

On the day we landed on Martinique, Lila and I decided to go by ourselves and take a bus to the wonderful national park called Jarden de Balata. We had a great time walking around the park, watching hummingbirds sip nectar from the plants, taking close up shots of dozens of flowers and filming their most magnificent plant, called bird of paradise, an appropriate name for a plant on this island of paradise. The flower of this plant looks just like a bird and has always been one of my favorites. At home in my greenhouse, I get a flower from my bird of paradise plant about once every two years. In the tropics of Martinique they bloom all the time. It was just magnificent to see those flowers in full bloom all around us.

We walked though the garden for hours and hours, but it seemed like a moment. Off in the distance were the mountains of the Martinique. They must have been just like Columbus saw during his voyages to the islands. I can imagine how he reported to King Ferdinand and Queen Isabella "how beautiful those Indies were." All of a sudden we realized that time had flashed by and we had but thirty-minutes until our vessel would be leaving for the next island.

We rushed out of the park to find a cab, but there was none in sight. We started walking in the direction of the port, but of course there was no chance of making it back to the boat on foot in less than thirty minutes. The thought that came to mind was whether we would have to fly to the next island if we missed the boat that night. Then luckily a bus came along and we jumped on board. For about twenty minutes we played "give and take" with the clock. At first, the bus made good time down a long steep road, then it slowed down to pick up passengers. At last we reached the town, but it was still a mile or two to the harbor. Would we make it or would we miss it? Then the bus finally arrived at the port as we saw the tender crew pulling up their lines about to leave for The Windstar riding peacefully at anchor out in the harbor. We raced to the boat and jumped on as the tender's ropes were thrown on board. We made it! From then on we decided to take an alarm watch with us when we traveled alone. As I sat in the tender watching the Windstar patiently waiting for our arrival, I thought to myself and wondered if any of Columbus's men ever missed their boats going back to Spain.

UNITED STATES/CANADA

2. Key West: A Favorite Picture

Since my European trip to Praque during the previous summer, 2001, I had not traveled further from home than Mystic, Conn. I was concerned that my back would experience another bout with the infection that I experienced the year before in Europe. But in 2002, I took a "kindergarten" trip to the southernmost spot in continental United States. I had been to Key West once about 15 years earlier, but I always wanted to go back especially since I read Charles Kuralt's book on his favorite twelve places in the United States.

The late CK spent a year traveling around the country, one month in each of his special places. He started his famous trip in January and guess where he went? You guessed it—Key West. He made it sound so wonderful that I have always wanted to see it in more detail.

So when I knew I would be in southern Florida the next winter, I thought Key West would be a great place to spend some time. A few weeks before we were going to travel to our apartment in Hallandale, I asked Joe if he would like to spend a few days in Key West. He said it would be great but that he may have a friend with him. I said that would be fine with me. The next week I picked up Joe and Bena at Ft. Lauderdale Airport. To my surprise, it turned out that I had met Bena when I visited New Paltz, New York the year before at a reading session at Evelyn's house. (Joe lived part time at Evelyn's house and she has periodic reading groups for readers and writers.) I enjoyed myself that evening and I remember sitting across from Bena and her friend, Ed, at Evelyn's pot luck dinner before the reading. Now here we were planning to take a trip together.

The three of us left about eleven on a Sunday morning for what was expected to be a three hour trip from Hallandale to Key West. By the time we arrived in Key West the trip took us almost five and one half hours. Route 1 (the highway that stretches from northern Maine to Key West, Florida) becomes a single lane road for almost the entire 130 miles from Key Largo to Key West. Because of a lot of traffic, we drove over the 41 bridges and dozen or so Keys at an unusually slow pace but we were not in a hurry and enjoyed the scenery. The Keys are naturally developed islands that were evolved by growing sand bars and bird droppings over a period of millions of years along the Florida Bay. It was hard to believe that these little islands gradually became inhabited by humans over thousands of years. We stopped off for lunch at one of the Keys called Upper Matacumber. We sat in the backyard of a cute little restaurant and enjoyed the wonderful smell of sea air. Next to the place was a dock that advertised "Feed the Tarpons for two dollars".

At the end of the 100-foot dock was a group of tourists looking into a big hole. After lunch we joined them. We watched the people tossing little fish to the tarpons in the water hole. The tarpon is a game fish about 6 to 9 feet long which is not good for anything but fighting and preying on other fish. After catching the tarpons the fishermen throw them back because they are too bony and muscular to be used for food. Alongside the tourists were dozens of pelicans that also tried to catch the little baitfish being tossed into the viewing hole.

The place was called Bobbies Dock and was advertised as being there for twenty-five years. I was intrigued how someone could make a lifelong living from this ingenious idea of building a dock with a hole at the end and sell the rights for people to look into the hole for one dollar. And for two additional dollars give them a small bucket of fish to throw into the hole and watch the tarpons jump up out of the water to catch the small bait. But seeing is believing and a lot of people did just that.

We joined the interested crowd who came all afternoon to watch the rather simplistic entertainment. Another part of the show was a very active dog that would chase the pelicans away. Every once in a while a pelican would dive into the hole to catch a little fish used as bait and one of the attendants would take a big net, catch the pelican and take it out of the hole. The whole show including the feeding of the tarpons, the flying pelicans and the dog chasing the pelicans cost a few bucks, and helped to make the five hour trip a little less boring—all of this because of what I call American ingenuity.

We arrived at the Marriott at sundown and barely had time to see the favorite interest in this part of southern Florida. What Key West offers for almost three hundred evenings of the year is a magnificent sundown. I told Joe and Bena that one evening we would take a boat out into the harbor to enjoy an exciting and beautiful sunset. Two citizens who helped to make Key West what it is today are Ernest Hemingway and Harry Truman.

One year Hemingway was on his way back from Cuba to the United Stated when a storm came up and his captain decided it would be a good idea to land on Key West and wait out the weather. After the storm subsided Ernest walked around the island and it became love at first sight. He loved the homes and the shops. Before he knew it, he bought a little house and stayed there for over twenty years. He often went back and forth between Key West and Cuba, which is only 90 miles apart, and loved the fishing waters between the two places.

Similarly, when President Truman was looking for a place to use for vacations, he picked Key West and during his Presidency of six and one half years he went there dozens of times because he loved the solitude of the spot. The Presidential record shows he spent 175 days in the "Key West White House". On our trip Joe and I spent several enjoyable hours walking around the beautiful house that Harry and Bess called their home for a while. It is simple and neat just like the Trumans were. It was an ideal home for an ideal President. Harry Truman was one of my favorite presidents and the first one for whom I had the honor to vote and for whom I had such admiration.

The next afternoon we walked around the old town, watching thousands of tourists pouring off four cruise ships that had anchored in the city's port for the day.

The restaurants were jammed and the tour buses and trolleys gave the people a running commentary of the history of Key West. The museums and the harbor sailing ships too were jammed to capacity. We drove all around the city that reminded me a little of New Orleans. The bars and restaurants were doing a thriving business. Several of the places were called "dress optional" (which was another form of strip shows, we found out), but we did not visit them. The music blasted out in the street until late at night. The streets were crowded with thousands of tourists watching other tourists and buying souvenirs for family members back home.

The next day we got up early to go to the beach but took time out to stop at the landmark buoy that is listed as the Southernmost spot in the continental United States. The place is crowded with even more tourists taking pictures of this landmark. Along the street are little kiosks with dark skinned people from Cuba selling T shirts and other memorabilia from their mother country. All along the road are hotels, rooming houses, bread-and-breakfast inns, each with signs like, "The Southernmost home in the USA or the "Southernmost motel in the country". The other attraction of the place is listed as, "only 90 miles from Havana, Cuba."

For history buffs, beside the Truman summer "White House", there is the Zachary Taylor Fort which was build in the middle of the nineteenth century. It was used to protect the country from a possible invasion from Mexico. One day we had a great time on the beach adjacent to the fort. Joe and Bena swam in the ocean and did some snorkeling. I stood by the ocean and reminisced about my days of swimming and snorkeling. I always feel sad about the things that I can no longer do because of my back. But then I rationalize—at least I am here to watch rather than not to be here at all.

After a busy day we raced back to get on the schooner that sailed off at exactly five o'clock for the sunset cruise. The ship, one of about ten, which leaves from the harbor to see the sun go down at 6:30 PM this time of year, Is a four mast schooner, called the Western Union. It has a crew of eight and 100 or so sightseers. When the masts are hoisted many more than eight men are required. The captain asked for volunteers to help pull up the sails. Surprising myself, I and some others volunteered with the lines. We actually worked hard to hoist the ropes. Joe said he did not think that I would be able to put forth so much effort hoisting the sails. It felt good to put in the effort and I enjoyed straining my muscles for a change.

It was a wonderful two-hour cruise, culminating in the sun slowly sinking below the horizon. Sometimes as the sun goes down you can see a flash of blue green light, although, this time we did not see it. As we headed back to the harbor, the shoreline was jammed with sightseers watching the sunset as we, the lucky ones, entered the harbor on our schooner.

I have seen many sunsets, in many different part of the earth and each one gives me a special kind of thrill. This one ended with a magnificent sailing ship passing right in front of the setting sun as we looked on from the deck of The Western Union. At that instant Joe took my picture, which turned out to be one of the best pictures I have ever had taken of myself. It is the one that I have used for the back cover of my first and second books.

As we sat around the desk looking at the skies and the other sailing ships around us, the crew handed out a cup of steaming hot Conch Chowder that just hit the spot. I began talking to the ships engineer, a man about 60 years old, who was an electronic engineer up north for his entire career. Then about five years ago, he gave up a great job and moved down to Key West to enjoy the climate and relaxed atmosphere. After a while he got itchy to do some work so he applied to become the ship's engineer aboard the Western Union. He had to learn all about inboard diesels and now he has become an expert in keeping the two Western Union engines with thousands of parts, up and operating.

As he told me his story we were arriving back at the pier where thousands of people seemed to be welcoming us into the harbor, or at least I thought so. All of a sudden what sounded like a large bomb going off turned out to be a beautiful display of fireworks. Then more and more of them went off. It was a magnificent show. I asked the engineer with whom I had been talking, "Is this show given every night? He said with a laugh, "Oh, no they just knew you were going to be here." Then, smilingly, he told me that there was a private party in the Billie Fish Bar and Grill restaurant. The family that hosted the party also paid to have the ship in the harbor shoot off those fireworks. He said that it was a better exhibition than either the Fourth of July or New Years Eve. I do not know how we happened to be in Key West on Feb 23, 2002 but we were lucky enough to see this wonderful show.

We arrived back at the Marriott after a long day and evening around this great little town. The next morning Joe decided to introduce Bena and me to a pawnshop viewing. Neither of us had ever been to a pawnshop before. But Joe went to pawn often, to look for musical instruments to buy, repair and resell. He took us to three pawnshops—all that Key West had. None of them had any instruments that interested Joe. But it was fun to look at the huge variety of items that a pawnshop has. From cue sticks to old cameras to toy fire engines, they had thousands of things to clutter up your house with. About the only transaction we made was that Joe bought a few CD's for $3.00.

On that last night, Joe and I had dinner at a little outdoor cafe while Bena took a walk along Caroline Street. Next to the restaurant was another man who had a unique way of earning a living. His whole stock-in-trade was two cameras (video and Polaroid) an iguana, two snakes and two parrots. For twenty dollars he took your picture with his camera after placing the snakes around your neck, the iguana in your lap and the parrots on your head. While Joe and I enjoyed our dinner, he collected one hundred and eighty dollars from nine tourists who wanted their pictures taken with this weird variety of animals. A great business, I thought, and they were all cash transactions—I am sure he had no payroll except for bird food and whatever snakes eat. I will bet that he filed no return on April 15th.

At last our trip to Key West would be coming to an end. As I thought back to all the interesting people we met: the guy at Bobbie's Dock and his twenty-five year old hole in the deck to lore tarpans; the engineer who fled from the north to become the diesel engineer aboard the schooner, Western Union; the camera man with his iquanas, two parrots and two snake and lastly, the three pawn brokers who could only interest us in CD's.

Key West was certainly an interesting place to visit. I could see why Harry Truman and Ernest Hemingway came back.

3. Murder at Marathon Key.....

At last our trip had come to an end and we made plans to leave for Miami about eleven the next morning. We believed that it would take us five hours as it had taken us that amount of time when we arrived. Joe wanted to get back about four so that he would be able to spend time with his brother that afternoon. It was a cloudy day and we did not believe that there would be too much traffic on the road.

We could not have been more incorrect. About one hour out of Key West the traffic came to a crawl and then almost stopped all together. We then went at an incredibly slow pace for what seemed to be hours. From then on, it took us almost two hours to get to Marathon that is a little over fifty miles from Key West. We could not get any idea what was the matter. But at long last we saw a dozen blinking lights on the road. It looked like it must have been an accident of some kind and that the road was closed. Joe who was driving made several attempts to get around the accident but the Keys are so narrow that we just could not get around the jam. We would always come back to Good Old Route 1 that is the only real road that one can take.

Finally we got into a Shopping Center in the heart of Marathon and saw a little restaurant called Deli and Dock and decided to stop for some lunch. Surprisingly we were the only ones there. The waitress took our order and said she is closing the place for the day. She was clearly very upset and although she tried to hide them, she had tears in her eyes. Seeing that something was very wrong, I asked her what was the matter. She hesitated for an instant until I asked her why there was such a tie-up on route 1. I never realized my two questions were very much tied together—"Why was there such a jam here in the little town of Marathon? And why was she so upset?"

She then told us her story. That morning at around eight-thirty as she was going to work, she stopped at the one traffic light in town. Then she continued with great emotion, "As I was waiting for the light to change I was just day dreaming about something or other. Then I heard the most terrific blast that I have ever heard in my life. The sound went throughout my entire body and it actually lifted me off the seat. It was horrible." She began sobbing as she pointed from her head to her toe to emphasis the fact.

"I looked in the direction of the car next to me," she said, "and saw the front half was almost entirely destroyed. The lady driver was slumped over the steering wheel and bleeding badly. I jumped out of my seat and opened her car door. I realized that I recognized this woman. She often came into this restaurant."

She pointed to a chair at an adjacent table. You could tell that she was picturing that poor woman sitting in this very place. She went on, "She was very badly hurt but I opened the door and pulled her out. I laid her out on the sidewalk."

She told us that the woman seemed very badly hurt, especially her leg, but she thought that she would live. She knew the victim was a nurse in her fifties, working in a local nursing home, and had just moved into Marathon about two months before. She wondered why someone put a bomb in her car. Then the waitress began to cry again as she told us that she just heard over the radio that the woman had died. We asked her why then was the road still closed so many hours later. Apparently, the police had closed the road on both sides waiting for the FBI to come from Miami. She said that the police had said that there could be another bomb in the car. As she talked we could see how very upset she was. She said that she was closing the place because she wanted to see her doctor to check out her hearing. The noise of the bomb blast was still ringing in her ears.

The story became more intriguing. Why was the FBI being called into this little innocent town half way between Key Largo and Key West? I thought just how much crime could possibly take place in this place. Our waitress gave us a little clue. She later told us that a phone call from a friend said the woman was going to be a witness at a trial soon and could possibly be the target of a hit by a gang. I thought at the same time that the victim may have been placed in a witness protection plan to keep her safe while she was waiting to be called. Apparently it did not work.

After lunch we left little old sleepy Marathon and headed back toward Miami. About an hour down the road we saw a caravan of cars with blinking red lights. We assumed that the people in them were the FBI going down to start the investigation. That night there was just a little information about a traffic jam on Route 1 in the Keys and that a woman had died in an accident. There was very little more information. It seemed to me the fact that there was so little information was suspicious in and of itself.

The entire trip took us almost eight hours and was an annoyance to all the travelers to and from the Keys, but to the nurse from Marathon it was terrible tragedy. Had we not stopped off in Marathon, that incident would have been nothing more than a traffic jam to us. Meeting that waitress in the restaurant and hearing of her tale made the "incident" much more alarming and personal. It is very rare that we have actual contact with someone who witnessed such a blast and murder. To share her story and the fright she experienced has never left me. I will never travel the road from Miami to Key West without thinking of that murder.

4. The Quiet, Running Everglades

In the past four years I have written about 60 travel stories as many of my readers know. Starting in Europe when I was still working I wrote about Germany, France, Greece and many others, Then I wrote about my trips to Africa, Asia, the Arctic and Australia and New Zealand. Most recently I have written about my trips to South America and Iceland. In essence I have written stories about every continent and at least fifty countries that I have visited in the past thirty years.

The one country that I have visited quite a lot but never wrote about is my own. Now that patriotism is running so high here at home. I feel it appropriate to write about the good old USA. I got to thinking of the many places that I have seen. In my early years, I went to Maine several times. I spent time along the coast from Boothbay Harbor to Bar Harbor. It is a beautiful state indeed. Some time I will write about it. Then I visited the Colorado

Rockies, the Grand Canyon and Bryce and Zion National Parks.

But the place that I have seen most and that I have a special spot in my heart, is Florida's Everglades. About the only time people hear of the Everglades is when there is a fire or some other natural disaster. The Everglades are not as spectacular as the western National parks or the eastern shore states. It has it's own special kind of beauty. It is completely flat, this river of grass with its alligators and wading birds and it's giant mosquitoes. The centerpiece of the Everglades is its river. One would never even think that the Everglades has a river because this unusual body of water is only about 6 inches deep but it flows ever so quietly from the Lake Okachobee to Florida Bay. It flows among the many tree hammocks and the tall fields of grass.

I have visited the Everglades about a half dozen times. All of my visits seem to blend into one. I went there with Lila and her sister and brother-in-law, Kiala and Al. I went there with Jeff our son-in-law and then with my cousin, Ilene. Each time we would go down to the tip of the park to take out a flat boat or canoe and ride among the lakes and streams or join a party boat with fifty or hundred park visitors. On one trip Jeff and I stayed over at a cabin overlooking the Florida Bay. This was especially memorable because of the incredible Sunset that we saw. I have seen sunsets from the Arctic to the southern tip of South America but standing on the edge of the Everglades is one that will remain in my mind as a very special one.

It was real clear and the sky was full of birds just as the sun was setting. Somehow birds seem to sense the setting of the sun and you could see them fly across the sky just as the sun was going down which made it extremely special. You feel as though you are at one with nature. It is a sky to remember.

The other thing that is memorable but not pleasant are the mosquitoes. I think that there are more mosquitoes in the Everglades than any place on earth (maybe with the exception of the New Jersey Shore). There also seems to be bigger-size mosquitoes in the Everglades than any place else. Even though we brought mosquito repellent, they attacked us in swarms. But it is all part of the Everglades experience. Whether one takes a boat out into the bay or a canoe into the lakes it is a trip to remember. One day while we were taking an excursion boat in the Florida bay we had a double treat. The captain pointed out a pair of mating turtles which we got very close to but not close enough to disturb their love making. A few minutes later we saw a manatee that does look like a mermaid. It is manatees that seaman took for "ladies of the sea" many centuries ago.

So from the smallest mosquito to the biggest manatee the Everglades is a place to visit. I am looking forward to going there soon again with Joe.

5. Savannah and Her Squares

One Sunday morning as I was watching my favorite program of the same name, Charles Osgood had a segment about Savannah's famous restaurant Wilkes Eatery. Madame Wilkes is a 94-year-old Southern lady who spent her entire career cooking good simple food. Lila and I were never fortunate enough to have enjoyed one of her meals but we did spend a few days in her warm and hospitable city during a trip around the South in the middle 1980s.

Savannah, Georgia to me is the quintessential southern city and the heart of the Southern United States. It was founded around the end of the eighteenth century by a group of Southern gentlemen led by James Oglethorpe.

Oglethorpe's philosophy was to lay out the city with 24 squares in the center, so that if attacked by the Indians, the neighbors of an area would be able to congregate in the center and defend themselves. Every few blocks he planned to have one of these square, so in essence, Savannah was the first planned city of the New World.

Gradually these city centers became parks and were dedicated to heroes of the nation and the south like Lafayette or Calhoun. In the nineteenth century beautiful stately homes were built around the squares. Many of them stood for the better part of a century, but in the depression some of the areas began to decay.

Fortunately some far-sighted citizens of the city realized how important it was to save the city centers and an all out effort was made to collect funds to protect the city squares. The result is a wonderful classic old city that, to me, is the most beautiful city in the south and arguably the entire nation. Maybe, Savannah is too formal and rigid for some tastes but to me it has a classic look that I love.

Early one morning I walked around, square after square, looking at so many elegant homes and churches that it was dizzying. My favorite was Savannah's Temple Mikvah Israel. it was on the corner of one of the squares called Monterey. It was a magnificent structure and the third oldest temple in the country. In the afternoon, Lila and I walked through it again. This time we were able to go inside and building was just as beautiful inside as it was on the outside.

In addition to the Temple we stopped at several homes that are now open to visitors at various times of the year. I think the most beautiful time to visit Savannah is the spring when the azaleas are in bloom. The South must have some of the most beautiful gardens in the world. Although every time I visit a different part of our planet, I say they have the most beautiful gardens. (I am very fickle about that).

Nevertheless, we visited Savannah in the spring and the gardens were truly gorgeous. Inside the homes, too, everything was very beautifully kept up or refurbished. The furniture was typically southern mahogany. Elegantly adorned were the dining rooms with Chinaware and glassware to remember a lifetime.

On the second day, I stopped off at a bookshop near River Street and predominately displayed right up in front was a recently written book about the city called "Midnight in the Garden of Good and Evil" by John Berendt. Naturally I bought a copy that was signed by the author who spent a part of his time in Savannah. The book describes the city with many of its colorful inhabitants. If you have not read it, I recommend it highly.

The city is not only squares and elegant homes. The original reason for its existence was its seaport. It is a well-protected harbor alongside the Savannah River several miles from the Atlantic Ocean. The seaport is still an area to visit with its newly decorated shops and hotels. It is a buzzing place especially at Christmas time. One of the wonderful shops to visit is the candle shop. They have hundreds of candles of every shape, smell, size and form. They are great gifts when you have run out of holiday ideas.

We walked along the waterfront during our stay in Savannah and watched the many freighters and leisure craft ply the river. We stopped off at the Hilton for lunch and had a front row table to enjoy watching the tourists strolling along River's Road. After lunch we were ready to continue our trip up North to New York and the still cool weather that is typical of our city in early April.

6. Historic Charleston

We left Savannah driving across the New Savannah River Bridge heading north to Charleston, one of the most historic and oldest cities of the deep South. I visited a Charleston suburb, Myrtle Beach, about fifteen years before when I was taking an executive management-training course. One of the great things about taking the Mahler Executive Management Training Program is that we got to visit many interesting cities. The program extended over a period of two years. Every quarter we would go to a different city studying a different aspect of management. It was one of the most important executive training programs that I ever took.

During the week in Charleston, we spent five days studying personal management. At the end of the week, the twelve of us, executives all, drove to Charleston for dinner and enjoyed the experience. We walked around Charleston for an hour or so before going back to the magnificent rented homes along Myrtle Beach that served as our school.

I knew that some day I wanted to go back to this famous city of the South. Now, Lila and I were here at last. We arrived in the early evening a long way from Myrtle Beach but right in the heart of Charleston. We found a local motel and turned in early; I was anxious to do some early morning sightseeing. The next morning I was out on the sightseeing trail. I started the walk down the famous Meeting Street. There are dozens of classic old homes each one is so different from the other. After awhile, I reached a beautiful old church, walked in and quietly sat in the rear pew. I realized that I was sitting where sat some of the most important gentlemen of the eighteenth and nineteenth century; even General Washington found time to visit this Charleston church. I left the church by the rear door to walk among the churchyard stones of such men as Calhoun and Clay. This is history.

Shortly after eleven o'clock, I took a cruise ship into Charleston Harbor. It was a thrilling ride out to Fort Sumter that rests on an island out in the harbor. This is one of the most famous of forts where the Civil War started. Our guide told us there were a few hundred Northern troops stationed at the fort that President Lincoln sent there to protect the rights of the Union. They where attacked by the Confederate forces from Fort Johnson, and so began one of the bloodiest wars in American history. I stood there gazing at the little fort and realized it was here where history was made.

After cruising around the fort, our ship passed up and down the Cooper River stopping off at the Charleston Naval Base. On the way back we passed by the battery of cannons that the confederates used to protect the city during the Civil War. We continued past the magnificent homes that the wealthy southerners lived in for the last one hundred years.

Then on the way back to the Ashley River, our little tour boat passed alongside the huge aircraft carrier, Yorktown. We gasped at the size of this gigantic vessel. Our guide told us that this aircraft carrier, ten times the size of our little boat was one of the hero warriors of WW2. It is anchored out in the harbor to remind old sailors like myself how the war in the Pacific was won by venerable ships, like this one. On the return voyage, we docked outside the famous old Naval Academy, the Citadel.

Traveling around the Charleston Harbor was a thrill of a trip indeed. In the afternoon I went back to classic Meeting Street, this time in a horse-drawn buggy of course, which drove us past many of the famous houses of the city. The driver with whip in hand, told us about each of the houses on either side of the street.

Most were between 150 and 200 years old, many were currently being refurbished. As our buggy drove by, we saw some homes being painted the same original colors of olden days. Most of the houses were beautifully kept and those that were not, would probably be cleaned up shortly. It was so nice to think that this city valued its history. One amusing fact I remember about Charleston is that the horses pulling the buggies wore diapers in order to keep the city streets clean. I wish that the horses in Central Park would wear them also.

The next day before setting out again for New York we drove out to the most beautiful gardens that I have seen on the East Coast. The Magnolia Gardens are about twenty miles from Charleston. They are over two hundred years old with beautiful magnolia trees, magnificent azalea and rhododendron sections that were absolutely breath taking. We expected to stay for an hour or so. But four hours later we were still walking around the magnificently tall oaks draped with Spanish Moss. These historic gardens attracted me like a bee to honey.

At sunset, we finally left for New York, reluctantly leaving Charleston with its history, glory and beauty and the fragrance of the flowering gardens still lingering with us.

7. Three Bonsai Gardens

It was the last stop of our twelve-day New England cruise from New York to Montreal in 2001. We had visited the cities of Newport, Rhode Island, Boston, Massachusetts, and Bar Harbor, Maine—three historic cities of New England. From there stopped at the historic city of Halifax on the island of Nova Scotia, and the idyllic small landing called Peggy's Cove. Later we docked at Sydney, Newfoundland on Cape Breton and visited the little towns of Baddeck (Alexander Graham Bell's summer home for 37 years) and Fort Louisberg. From there we spent a day at one of the most beautiful of the Eastern Canadian Provinces, Prince Edward Island.

Then our cruise ship headed southwest down the St. Lawrence River and through the Saginaw Fjords, finally arriving at the two major bilingual cities of Canada, Quebec and Montreal. It had been an exciting trip with a memory a day to write about. But here we are coming to the end of the journey.

In our hotel room in Montreal I looked through the tourist literature of Montreal. There was an article about that city's Botanical Gardens. It stated that Montreal had a larger variety of interesting bonsai plants than any place outside of Asia. I had seen bonsai plants in China and Japan. They were spectacular indeed. There were pines less than 20 inches high and over five hundred years old. I loved the gardens in Suchou and Hangchou. Then there were the Japanese plants in Kyoto.

I was intrigued to think that Montreal could have a comparable collection. I knew that Montreal's botanic gardens would be one of our last stops and, I believed too, it would be something to remember. Sometimes one just hits a home run without even trying. Our day at the botanic gardens was such a hit. What was so special about our day in the gardens? I will enjoy telling you.

Joe and I arrived at the gardens, at around 11:00 A. M. on a weekday morning. The place was all but empty. We had taken the Montreal Metro from downtown Montreal to the Biosphere stop and had to walk about a mile to get to the Botanical gardens. It was difficult walking for me but the thought of the gardens kept me going. Fortunately when we got inside the park there was a tram to take you from one section to another. That tram made the day possible for me. We took a tram from the entrance of the park to the Chinese section and got off at stop No. 2. From there we had to walk the last two hundred yards. It seemed as though it took forever. As we got closer I started to see posters announcing the Chinese lantern show, I thought it only would be in the evening. Then all of a sudden it hit us. There we were in the midst of thousands and thousands of the most colorful silk lanterns all around a man-made lake. It was spectacular beyond belief. In the lake there must have been a dozen brightly colored silk boats. At the edge of the lake there were Chinese fishermen so lifelike that you would almost believe they were real. Along the paths there were animals from cows to tigers, dogs, rats, monkeys and many others from the Chinese calendar: all life size and all made from brightly colored silk. There were reds and oranges, yellows, greens and blues. They looked so real that one could be convinced they were alive.

.Joe and I walked around the lake in awe for well over an hour. As usual I was glad we had not gone on a tour because a typical guided tours would have given you twenty minutes to see the whole place. On the opposite end there was a man-made miniature mountain, which we climbed up on to look down on the lake and its silken inhabitants. The entire scene was so beautiful as to be surreal. There we were expecting to see wonderful bonsai plants and we discovered this fabulous Chinese Lantern Exhibit. It was only in Montreal for ten days and we were lucky enough to be there during that time. As we walked around the lake my back pain and fatigue melted away with the excitement of what we were seeing.

Then we left the lantern exhibit and spent another hour visiting the remainder of the Chinese bonsai garden. They also, were spectacular, but after seeing the Chinese lanterns they were not quite as colorful. We had to rethink our appreciation of what we had seen and were about to see. The entire Montreal botanical gardens have three sets of bonsai plantings, each magnificent in their own way—the Chinese, Japanese and Western conifer.

The Chinese bonsai plants were up to several hundred years old. They were spectacularly knurled and very interestingly dwarfed. They were so special and interesting. Then we came upon the Japanese Bonsai Gardens. They had the very special flavor of Japanese simplicity and uniqueness. I thought they were the most beautiful. Joe and I just loved walking the Japanese sections—inside, through many rooms of Japanese bonsai plants and outside, around the gorgeous lake edged with so many plants. Joe and I agreed this definitely was the most beautiful bonsai garden ever.

That was until we reached the western conifer plantings that were incredibly beautiful and extremely unusual. They were set on a sandy and rocky terrain with dozens of breathtaking bonsai. We walked around looking at scores of pines, maples, junipers, cedars and many more, each listed with its type, age and place of origin. Some of them were as old as six hundred years. The western conifer area had bonsai, which made the territory appear to be a miniature western plateau. One ancient plant looked as if it would not last another year. There was only one small branch remaining from a once vibrant bonsai, but it was already 575 years old so who was I to know how long that branch would remain alive. I thought to myself that even ancient bonsai get old. I could not believe that some of them existed before Columbus discovered America. These were naturally miniature due to their surroundings and must have lived for hundreds of years in the western part of our country prior to being transplanted to Montreal. We studied these in awe; they were my favorites.

We took the tram back to spend a while viewing once again those gorgeous Japanese Gardens. They had a magnificent lake that was so calm and peaceful that Joe and I just stood there for minutes on end. We took dozens of pictures around a little man-made lake surrounded by scores of lilies. It is one of those sights that will stay with me for as long as I will remember. Then slowly we retraced our steps to the Chinese section. It too was just as spectacular as the first time with the colorful silk figures reflecting upon the water of the gorgeous lake. We walked around quietly enjoying every serene setting. All three of them had their own very special kind of beauty, but as a final thought I must say, the most impressive part of the very impressive day was the walk around the Chinese man-made lake with its hundreds of oriental lanterns from a world nine thousand miles away.

As I think back at the advertisement that drew us to the Botanical gardens that day, stating that Montreal had the most and best Bonsai Gardens outside of Asia, I now believe it.

8. Quebec—The Old Town

I was completely taken by the old city of Quebec. You see I am really jealous. Although I live in one of the oldest cities on our continent, my great frustration is why it doesn't look that way. When we got off the ship I was immediately taken with the Old Town of Quebec. If I closed my eyes and opened them again I could have been transported oceanographically and chronologically to the picturesque city of Paris three or four hundred years ago. The old buildings in the Royal Square could have been in any of a dozen squares in Ole Paris. In the center of the square is a bust of Louis XVI. Around the square are dozens of old buildings from the eighteenth century. At the opposite end from whence we entered the square, is the Notre Dame church. We entered the church and felt as tough we were transported back to an age long ago. We could have been seamen coming off a cruise from a sailing ship in the 1750's. In the entrance of the church hanging from the ceiling was a model of a four-mast sailing vessel. The model, we were told, was over three hundred years old but in perfect condition.

To think that with a little foresight New York could have left many old squares south of Wall Street instead of reconstructing the artificial South Street seaport with its modern mall and department stores. 'New' York has taken that first word in its name too seriously. Everything has to be 'New'. We destroyed Lower New York. Then wiped out 19th-century classic Fifth Avenue and most recently did a job on Pennsylvania Station. (We finally learned to save Grand Central Station with the help of Jaclyn Kennedy Onassis)
But by that time it was much too late. Almost everything relative to everyday living in the eighteenth century is destroyed.

Before we arrived in Quebec, I thought that all major cities in North America were as stupid as New York. I thought that most other cities had destroyed their classic old heritage. But then I was introduced to Quebec. What a beautiful little city is their "Old Town"! The outside of every building in Old Town cannot be changed. Every storefront, every roof, every little nook and corner of Old town cannot be varied. Even the color of the original tiled roofs representing the old families of the seventeenth and eighteenth centuries cannot be changed. The only compromise to modern technology is the tram to Upper Terrace (there is still an old walkway for the young and hardy). After walking around the Old Town and visiting Notre Dame, we took the tram to the newer city and the magnificent Chateau Frontenac.

We walked the length of the terrace to the beginning of the Plains of Abraham where Generals Wolfe and Montcalm both were killed on the same day in the most famous North American battle that the French and British had ever fought. I think, if the French had known how pretty Quebec would turn out, they would have fought harder. In any event we started walking up to the Citadel where the battle had been fought. We ascended about eight flight of steps when we met a couple coming down who told us that we had barely walked one quarter of the distance to the top of the fort. After thinking how much more I would have to walk, we turned around and headed back to the terrace of the Chateau Frontenac. It was built over many years and there are at least four different outside designs. Somehow the architecture all seems to fit together and its location is as dramatic as the building structures. The chateau is the center of all things beautiful in downtown Quebec.

After lunch we decided to go back to the ship for a rest. It was in the taxi that we met Leo, who spoke English as well as French as most taxi drivers do. He said for sixty dollars Canadian (forty US dollars), he would show us around the city the next day. We took him up on it.

The next day he picked us up as scheduled and drove us all over the city. One of the highlights that he liked best was the artistic Graffiti drawings that many so-called artists painted along the ramps leading to the highways. Instead of the New York's concept of cleaning off all traces of graffiti, the Quebec graffiti artists draw beautiful paintings that will probably stay for years.

Leo then took us to the Citadel to see the old fort by car instead of going there by foot as we attempted to do the day before. The Citadel is a huge fort build by the British in the middle of the 19th century at the edge of the Plains of Abraham. It is a five pointed fort with each corner designed to protect the two adjacent sides. But of course it never saw action since the Americans and the British have not been enemies since the War of 1812.

The next day, we took a bus tour fifty miles outside of Quebec where we saw two landmarks: one man-made and the other natural. The man-made structure is a beautiful cathedral, Saint Anne de Beaupre, sponsored by two fishermen who were in their boat but in deep trouble during a storm. They said that if they survived they would build a church dedicated to people in need.

Along the route were miles of pretty little homes no two alike. The driver pointed out the hundreds of unique window treatments in the houses. On the way we also saw many little chapels prior to reaching the beautiful structure dedicated to people who had physical handicaps and would go to the church to pray. In the back of the cathedral is a huge gallery of crutches and canes and other ambulatory aids from people who apparently left them after being cured of their ailment. As we approached the church the bells began to chime for what seemed to be a very long time. I thought it had some significance but it was just the daily one o'clock ringing.

The natural treat that we viewed was the Mont Morency Falls just outside of Quebec City. The falls are twice as high as Niagara but not nearly as wide. There is a walking bridge over the falls and a path winding down each side (the bridge swayed somewhat but not as much as the swinging bridge in Leshan, China over the Yangtze River). We walked across the bridge and part way down one side. We took pictures as we wound our way down the dirt path while the spray from the falls reminded us how near we were to these two-hundred foot high marvels of nature. It was truly spectacular.

We drove back to center of the city and returned to the ship satisfied that our visit to Quebec was all that we expected it to be. Quebec City is not a big place. It is less than one quarter the size of Montreal. But I will remember always the Old Town and the terraced upper city with the Chateau Frontenac in the center. Its beauty is something I'll never forget.

9. Traveling in Groups

As I have traveled all over the world, I often had the opportunity to go in groups. Going in groups has the advantage of having to do less planning for yourself but on the other hand there are distinct disadvantages. Generally, I prefer to travel with my friend, close relative or a friend or two. This story, however, describes vividly one of those disadvantages of group travel.

About ten years ago when I was a consultant to a small software company I went to Palm Springs, California, to participate in a conference where we were trying to sell a new programming product. For three days several of us stood in this huge conference center talking to dozens of potential customers, with very little success. It was a very frustrating effort.

On the last day I decided to sneak off and visit a State Park just outside of Palm Springs. It was the last afternoon of the show and I have always tried to take some time off and see a local attraction if possible. I drove ten or fifteen minutes into a magnificent deep forest with beautiful overhanging trees. It was high up on a mountainside that had an elevator that took us to the mountain top. At the top, we were greeted by a tour guide who showed us the lovely picturesque garden.

The tour into the forest took about an hour or so returning us to the elevator and then dropped us back to the hustle and bustle of the city below.

Just as I reached the elevator to descend, another group came off with the leader carrying the famous tour company banner called 'Tauck'. Tauck is wonderful company that advertises how many places they will take you to in just a few days. There among the group was an old friend from our condominium in Florida. The two of us immediately recognized each other and began to reminisce about our experiences in Hallandale. Leon was the president of our condominium and he immediately started to tell me with great emotion what was going on with our neighbors. He told me who had moved out and who had died and what problems they were having with the swimming pool. Since I had not been there in six months it was fun to listen to all the gossip.

You may ask what all this has to do with traveling alone or in groups. Although I have traveled all over the world I have very rarely taken a group trip. One does not have control of the time and location if one is part of a group. This story is a great example.

Leon and I talked for what seemed for just a few minutes but must have been much longer. All of a sudden I realized the sun was beginning to lower in the sky and I said to Leon that I would like to say goodbye. As I was saying this, I saw Leon's group heading back toward the elevator just as there leader said. "OK everyone back into the elevator."

Leon said with consternation, "Wait, I have not seen the Park yet."

The leader said, "Too late, we are going down now. We have to get back to our hotel as we have dinner in an hour."

And so proves my point—be prepared for tight schedules when traveling in a group. If you can adjust to group travel, then it's okay. I can't.

10. The Many Views of The Golden State

Joe and I arrived in Oakland on the afternoon of the first day of our trip to Northern California in 2002. Both of us could not get over the expansion of the airport. In the twenty years since our first arrival, the Oakland International Airport had expanded about ten fold. We had to take one of about twenty buses for a ten-minute ride to get to the car rental area. In the old days, there was Hertz, Avis and National. Now there must have been al least ten car rental companies some of which I had never heard before. We had a reservation with one called Dollar. Of course it cost much more than a dollar. The most interesting variation was the sign that read "bring back the car with a full tank of gas or you will be charged $6.00 per gallon for all the gas your vehicle needs. Now, that is inflation! It reminded me of the prices for gasoline one pays in Europe. In any event, Joe and I were careful to fill up our tank on the day we left California.

The first day we spent sightseeing around the Berkeley area where Joe had spent ten years of his life refurbishing houses.
He drove me to four homes some of which were built from fifty to hundred years ago. He lovingly showed me how he replaced foundations under homes, put on new sidings, roofs of these homes. In those ten years Joe got to know every part of a house and how to refurbish it. As we drove around Berkeley, it reminded me of a section in Brooklyn known as Flatbush, New York where I lived sixty years ago during my teenage days. All the homes were unique in that they were two or three stories high and the outsides varied in personality as the people who lived there.

I told Joe how World War II changed all that when a man named Levit began to build homes for millions of men coming back from the war as they needed housing in a hurry. Then during the next fifty years the words 'tract' and 'development' came into the building vernacular and homes were built by the score. That first evening we drove past a street near the University that is the most famous, or should I say infamous, street in Berkeley, called Telegraph Ave.

As we drove through the area I grabbed my video camera. On either side of the street were scores of little stands with bearded older men selling old cloths, used records and a variety of other things. It has been over a decade since I visited Telegraph Avenue. Our daughter, Sharon, lived in Berkeley back then and she took us to this famous street to absorb its unique atmosphere. What is so very different is the age of the people selling on the street. The beards are white and all the ladies have dyed blonde hair. But they still look just as far out and wildly dressed as they did back in the eighties.

It was fun to drive by and would have been fun to walk through but I too have changed a lot since the eighties and it is a lot harder for me now to walk down the street than I did years ago when I was with Sharon and Lila.

The next morning before starting out for Yosemite National Park that was to be the highlight of the trip, Joe and I decided to take a few days to visit friends and family. The first stop was to visit our cousins, David Sprung and Barbara Sprung Wilkes in San Francisco. They were scheduled to play in a concert in the Victorian Englander House and we were lucky enough to be in the right place at the right time. What a wonderful opportunity to see two of our most talented cousins perform.

Joe had developed many friends in the Bay area in his decade there, but I, too, had many family and friends I wanted to see. By proper planning our trip worked out perfectly.

While Joe went off to meet friends while I visited other cousins, Joe and Max-ine Berzok who left New York about a decade ago and now live in Oakland in a beautiful apartment overlooking the Oakland Lake which was once an estuary. It was wonderful to see them again. We went into Oakland's China Town to enjoy an authentic Chinese dinner. I visited old friends with whom I worked at General Instruments in the California division. I managed a big operation of almost one thousand people and George Oeh and Don Linden were part of my organization. We had lunch together to talk over the old times. It was a nostalgic afternoon.

In Berkeley, Joe and I stayed at the Claremont Hotel that had a hundred-year-old classic spa that was really worth visiting. Many of the rooms had been refur-bished and were absolutely gorgeous.

Then it was off to Yosemite, and the wonderful park. As we drove to the park—a three-or four-hour trip—we passed by hundreds of homes which had been built up into the very edge of the Berkeley hills, with magnificent views. Joe told me, however, how a good rainstorm would carry a few of these houses down from the hills every so often.

The city view gradually changed to rolling farms and meadows until we began to see the mountains of the Sierra Nevada. Up we climbed until our ears began to pop with the altitude. Then at last we reached the little town of Fish Camp that is just outside of Yosemite. Four hours of driving took us from the city life of Ber-keley and Oakland to the incredible beauty of Yosemite.

11. California's Garden of Eden

Forty miles from Yosemite Valley is one of the most beautiful places on earth. The Mariposa Groves contain some of the most magnificent Sequoia red woods found anywhere. Joe and I started out on our Yosemite National Park in this secluded section of the park. We drove out along Route 140 from Berkeley to Route 41 and came into the park from the South. It was five o'clock as we arrived and went immediately into the Redwood forest. Unfortunately we could not get a room in the park itself so we registered in the Tenaya Lodge. The three in-park hotels, The Ahwahnee, The Yosemite Lodge and the Wawona Lodge all required from nine months to a year for reservations. Since we only decided to go three months before we had to reserve a room at the Tenaya. It is three miles from the park on the South side but was a very acceptable hotel. The Tenaya was built about three years ago and has over two hundred great rooms at one half the price of the Ahwahnee. The big drawback is that it is thirty-five miles from the valley. But the big advantage is, it is right near the Mariposa Grove.

Since the Grove was so close we decided to go there first. We arrived at 5:15 P. M. in the evening to be told that the last tram goes out at 5:00 o'clock. We walked around the first section of the Grove for about a half hour only to realize that I could not hike Mariposa with my bad back. By the time I walked up to the Monarch tree my pain reached the level of six (on the one to ten pain scale).

We concluded that the smart way to see Mariposa was by tram which we took at ten the next morning. Nevertheless on the evening of the first day we arrived in Yosemite we saw a breathtaking view of Mariposa just before dark. The Sequoias were so huge that they seemed to take your breath away. The trees' barks are a gorgeous deep red and crystal clean like no tree I have ever seen. We are told one of the reasons the trees live so long is that their barks brush off any foreign matter and hence are so clean. The birds, insects and any outside matter seem to be brushed off from their bark leaving this bright red magnificent sound-resonating bark, like no other I have seen in my life. It is one thing to look at a red wood from afar but when I got up close I had a feeling there is something special that no one had ever told me about. It is the drum-like sound I heard when I pounded against certain parts of the tree. I never realized that the redwoods could resonate with a deep sound. Joe and I played the bark of one red wood as though it were a drum—a rather special experience.

One of the first trees that we saw was in fact a dead tree called the Monarch, and one of the most popular trees in the forest. It lays on its side in a peaceful repose for what some people say has been well over three hundred years. At its side was a picture taken in 1899 with a troop of one hundred Army Cavalry men on horseback sitting on its remaining two hundred foot length (one hundred feet of its top had been cracked off when it fell). What an impressive sight! The tree, because of its ability to withstand infection and decay, is estimated to have lived over twenty-five hundred years until the snow and ice finally toppled it to earth.

On the following morning Joe and I took one of the first trams deep into the Mariposa. The first stop was at one of the most popular places of all. It was at the California Tunnel tree, a huge redwood over two thousand five hundred years old that was burrowed out one hundred years ago so that a wagon would drive though its center.

As I stood at its center I thought of its ancient age. When this tree was a sapling, Alexander the Great, one of my favorite travelers, was still one hundred years away from being born. The tree was 500 years old when Julius Caesar lived.

When Marco Polo went to China, the tree was well over fifteen hundred years old and a dozen feet in diameter.

We continued our tram ride around the Grove. To get an idea of the vastness of the place, I asked one of our guides how many of the trees are over one thousand years old. He thought for a moment and then said, "I suppose almost three hundred trees"

In other words, I said, "This grove actually existed over one thousand years ago. He even seemed impressed as he said, "yes, I guess it existed pretty much as it does today."

"I suppose that by the time Columbus discovered America" I said, "This place was just like it is now."

Our guide answered, "Sure enough. One might say that. Five hundred years is just a drop in the bucket for a red wood."

Speaking of drops in a bucket, each mature redwood requires over ten thousand gallons of water a day, about the amount of water used in our swimming pool every single day. The root system to soak up so much water is about one hundred fifty feet in diameter. The sequoias wonderfully adapted to our planet. They survive forest fires and even grow better with fires every twenty or so years. They also grow well when transplanted in various other warm areas on earth.

In the nineteenth century, botanists took over three thousand seedlings from Yosemite National Park and replanted them in New Zealand, China and southern Russia. They all are thriving extremely well and growing, although rather slowly.

One thousand years from now, those countries will have extremely beautiful redwood forests. I cannot wait to see them.

12. Yosemite—Half Dome from Many Angles

Before I left home I made a list of the five most important highlights to see when I visited Yosemite National Park. At the top of the list was a visit to the Sequoia redwood trees in Mariposa Grove. On the first day of the trip, Joe and I spent hours in what I like to call a 'Garden of Eden'. In second place, but not too far behind, was the magnificent and shapely mountain called Half Dome. Its configuration and coloring absolutely intrigued me.

On day two we left our hotel called Tenaya Lodge, and headed for Yosemite Valley and Half Dome, a distance of about forty miles. It was a bright day with a perfectly clear, deep blue sky. We drove in silence passing miles of pines with their green hues that complimented the blue of the heavens. As we drove along I wondered when would I get my first view of Half Dome.

After almost one hour of driving we suddenly entered a tunnel. The tunnel was about a mile long so Joe turned on the car's bright lights. Finally, we came out into the brightness of the day. There in front of me was my first view of paradise. The sight was too spectacular for words. We were standing in full view of Half Dome with its perfect circular shape. Its name is meant to capture the mountain's appearance of having been cut in half.

The panoramic view of Half Dome included the neighboring granite marvel, El Capitan ('The Captain' in Spanish), the deep green pines of Yosemite Valley, and majestic gleam of the water coming off the five-hundred-foot Bridal Vail Falls is absolutely spectacular. I have never seen such scenic beauty in one magnificent sweep.

At the side of the road we stopped next to fifty other cars to enjoy the view by a signpost that read 'Tunnel View'. This name was an understatement if I ever heard one. I have rarely seen such an incredible view. One hardly ever sees so many picturesque images in one panorama. Later in the valley I noticed many familiar scenes photographed by photographers and artists. I took videos and Joe took stills to our hearts content. After the panoramic video I took a sweep of the bronze placard that described the scene in detail. I did not want to forget even the slightest element of this unbelievable scene. My first view of Half Dome thrilled me to the bone. We were almost speechless. All I could repeat was, "What a view!"

What I did not know was that there was so much more to come. We drove along the road for about a half hour to another area called Glacier Point that my guidebook listed as the number one scenic spot for a total view of the valley. I thought to myself, Could there be yet another spot more beautiful than Tunnel View? The answer would come shortly.

On the road to Glacier Point four or five buses were returning to the valley. I was glad we came before the busy season.

When we arrived the area was crowded with parked cars, and Joe dropped me off as close as possible to the Point. A directional sign stated 'one-quarter mile to the Glacier Point'. I started walking slowly while Joe looked for a parking place. My back was hurting quite a bit that day. As I began the walk, I asked a ranger how far to the point, not believing the quarter-mile sign. He said. "There is a good view about one hundred yards down the road to the right. You can see quite a lot from there."

I think he noticed my cane and limp, and probably thought I could not make it all the way to the Point itself. Joe joined as I reached the midway point the ranger referred to. The scene including Half Dome and Nevada and Vernal Falls was quite beautiful and we stopped to take videos of it all. Joe told me that this scene reminded him of his camping trip to Half Dome about twelve years earlier. He described the hike up to the falls and over the bridge behind them. I listen attentively, as Joe recalled the many details, and I thought what a great hike this would have been in my younger days. For now I was glad that I got as far as I had.

Then Joe continued to tell me how he walked out almost to the ledge and thought about peering over the side. Again I was with him every step of the way. He told me how he carefully crawled on the ground to the very edge. I shared his anxiety as he talked about reaching the last inch and looking down into the valley a mile below. I thought to myself, if I had only been here thirty years ago. But, alas, as I stood there now, I questioned if I could walk the last few hundred yards to Glacier Point. We all have our own struggles. I had just taken a pain pill and I was hoping that it would help take me there.

I asked a man coming back from the point if it was a difficult walk and was it worth it. I was hoping that he would say, "Don't bother. It is just like this spot." But his enthusiasm was very clear. "It is a fantastic view," he said, "especially the view of Half Dome and the Upper and Lower Falls."

That settled it. I decided that if I could make it to the bottom of the Pyramids in Egypt, and Joe could creep up to the edge of Half Dome, I was capable of walking the last four hundred yards to the lookout from Glacier Point. Fifteen minutes later I reached the edge of Glacier Point to see the magnificent views of Half Dome, the Village of Yosemite, and the Yosemite Falls the most gorgeous falls outside of Niagara Falls that I have ever seen.

Before we headed back to Berkeley, we drove again through the Valley on the last day. We walked at a leisurely pace on yet another swinging bridge spanning across the Merced River. This swinging bridge again could not be compared to the one we crossed in Leshan, China that hovered precariously fifty feet above the river. But in a few minutes we would have our last opportunity to experience Half Dome.

We drove to a beautiful place called Mirror Lake. It was the closest I would come to Half Dome. Mirror Lake is almost at the base of the mountain and gets it name from the reflection of the dome into the water. Joe took a brisk walk by himself while I wandered around taking videos of the mountain and the lake, and watched kids jump into the freezing water from the millennium-old boulders.

From this point in Mirror Lake, I could look almost straight up at Half Dome, a very different angle indeed. From every angle, Half Dome was a thrill for me to see.

Our trip to Yosemite was coming to a close now and my last view of this very interesting mountain that had been split in two by a glacier some 50 million years ago would have to stay with me for my lifetime.

13. Yosemite—El Capitan's Diamonds

I was home for a month now, but I still had Yosemite in my blood.

Every few days I would look at the pictures of Yosemite from Glacier Point or the Tunnel View. The beauty and grandeur of the valley floor still touched me. I would look at my pictures and have wonderful memories of our four days at Yosemite. One day our pool maintenance man, Robert Settle, came to clean our pool.

We recognized each other from last summer and he asked me "How was your year? You were going to France when I saw you last."

I told him that I did, but recollecting my recent thoughts, I said, "I just got back from Yosemite less than a month ago."

His face lit up as he said, "Oh, my Gosh! That's my favorite place. I have been there a dozen times. On one of my trips to Yosemite, I had the most exciting experience I have ever had. It was in October and a few of us were camping out near Tuolamah Meadows. I remember that night although it was over twenty years ago."

"What made it so memorable?" I asked.

"You know how the Rockies are made of granite?" he continued, "Well, it was the night of a full moon and as we lay on the ground, we suddenly saw the light from the moon creep up along the surface of El Capitan. Just before we could see the moon itself, the rays of light splashed upon the mountain like nothing I have ever seen and the granite looked like a billion sparkling diamonds. Have you ever seen a mountain sparkle like that? What a sight!"

He took a deep breath, and then said, "Gradually, the entire mountain came alive with brilliant shimmering stones. As the moon came up over the mountains it lit up the entire Yosemite Valley as though it were daylight. Then the moon reflected upon the Merced River and its reflection on its surface was too spectacular for words. I remember the air being very clear that night so everything I saw was so especially distinct. In the past twenty years I have traveled all over the world, but I still remember that October night as no other."

By this time Robert had finished vacuuming my pool. I felt as though I was back in Yosemite reliving my wonderful trip. His vision of El Capitan and how he described it is one I shall never forget. anyone who can remember all those details after twenty years is entitled to use the word 'unforgettable'. Robert and I said goodbye and as he left, I thanked him for sharing with me yet another view of El Capitan and Yosemite.

14. Washington: Remembered & Rediscovered

For my 78th birthday I decided to take some of my family to our Capitol, Washington D.C. It has been almost fifteen years since I visited that beautiful city. Years ago before I retired I would go to Washington almost once a month because we had so much business there. But when I would talk about going to Washington in those days it was more like going to a business district called Crystal City. Our General Instrument office was in a section known as Crystal Plaza, and our Navy customers were all over the area in Crystal City depending on which branch of the Navy we would be dealing with. Over the twenty or so years since I started doing business with them, the Navy had moved its headquarters from the center of Washington to the edge of Virginia. There were many times I would go to Washington and never set a foot in the great city.

About the only contact I would have was visual when the shuttle in which I was traveling would fly over the city, and I would get a marvelous view of the Washington monument, the Lincoln Memorial and the Capitol building. The approach into Washington National Airport would take me over the Potomac River and those three magnificent structures would be on our left side as we came in for a landing. I would try to get a window seat and when we would approach on a clear day, I would have my face right up against the window, like a kid on his first flight to enjoy every minute of that gorgeous sight.

But now it was three-quarters of a generation later and I wanted to take anyone of my family who could get away, to share the many new views and my remembrances of the old days.

The first memorial from the new series of memorials they have been building the last decade is the Franklin Delano Roosevelt Memorial. We took a taxi to the Tidal basin and walked the two hundred yards or so to the entrance to President Roosevelt's Memorial. Instead of being a single structure like the Lincoln or Jefferson Memorials, it is a series of areas giving one a chance to recall this formable president's important contributions during his lifetime. One of the most controversial of the scenes is seeing FDR sitting in his wheelchair. As I walked through the area, I can recall the days when I would listen to his resounding voice telling us that we have nothing to fear but fear itself.

He was my favorite leader in my youth and he gave us such reassurance that we thought of him as a father as well as a leader and president. As I stood there I realized that there are not many people left who actually remember his vibrant dynamic personality. It was a great experience to have the power of his voice

Our children ran around the various open air-rooms and looked at the radio of the type we had in our living room sixty years ago. I explained to them how television did not exist then

They looked at me in disbelief, "No television." they repeated. "No television," I said.

We spent two hours walking around the areas, from the terrible depression to the even more traumatic World War II. I relived my youth that seems now so very far away.

We left the FDR Memorial and walked to the World War II memorial at the edge of the reflecting pool that stands between the Lincoln Memorial and Washington Monument. It is a large amphitheater with fifty-six little marble steps representing each of the states and territories. In the center is a large water display and on either side is a memorial to the Atlantic and Pacific areas of Warfare. It was pretty visually but not meaningful to the war itself. The only part of the exhibit that actually touched me was the six bronze plaque which told the picture story of a group of soldiers from their enlistment to the their final battle. To me they could have done without the rest of it.

We left the WW II memorial and headed toward the Vietnam Wall. The long distance gave me time to think of those many years when the Navy Department had its huge 'temporary' headquarters along Constitution Ave. Those buildings must have been built during the First World War and remained along the reflecting pool there until the sixties when they were taken down, as very unappealing 'eye sores' in this otherwise very pretty city.

Now along Constitution Ave is a series of gardens, which probably will be used to honor some future president or war.

I watched as Matthew and Rachel walked alongside the Vietnam War Memorial—the black long remembrance to the 58,000 men and women who gave their lives in the terrible prelude to the current conflagration. Why is that so meaningful to me? It individually honors each and every person who was sacrificed in the war, not just presidents or battlefields, but also the very people themselves in a place where their families and loved ones can go to remember the sacrifice that the service men and women made for their country. Along the base were letters and stories, some just recently written, from the people who were touched directly by the loss. Rachel bent down alongside Lila, picked up one and read it aloud as Matthew hugged the wall with such feeling. We walked farther along the wall as Rachel read other notes and Matthew continued touching the wall. It was a moment I will long remember.

By this time I was so tired that I felt all my 78 years and we took a cab back to the hotel for a much needed rest. I would continue my travels tomorrow.

THE END

FDR: A Man For All Ages

Matthew, Rachel and Lila studying the Vietnam Memorial

EPILOGUE

Traveling around the world is an adventure that compares to no other. Visiting peoples from all ways and walks of life gives one a perspective that is awe-inspiring and enlightening to the soul.

I imagine that my four heroes of the civilized world—Alexander the Great, Julius Caesar, Marco Polo and Columbus must have experienced the same thrill.

Alexander was a very young man, the son of a very ambitious father, when he started out on his adventures to Persia and then all the way to India. I can imagine his thrill when he left Greece and made his way east to Persia and then for ten years he battled the greatest armies of the time until he finally reached India. At first he thought of going further, all the way to China, but his generals discouraged him because he they heard of an army of giants his mere human soldiers could not defeat. Later historians understood that what Alexander's generals were referring to was an enemy mounted on elephants. No doubt that would have been formidable indeed.

Although he lived to only thirty-two, his life must have been filled with so many exciting moments. I can imagine the thrill of the adventure as he walked through the streets of Greece and Turkey and traveled across the Mediterranean and down the Nile. Alexander and his men must have experienced great excitement in Egypt where he met the civilizations of the pharaohs that already existed for two thousand years.

Then five hundred years later came the Holy Roman Empire and the rulers from that millennium that set out to capture the West. Julius Caesar was the most powerful and greatest of all. He traveled west claiming France, Germany, Spain and others, then finally England to develop those areas to his liking. Now as I travel throughout these countries, I see the wonders he bought to these places.

I have enjoyed such fun and excitement visiting all the places that Caesar lead his men and letting my imagination wander. Especially inviting to me were the towns in southern France, like Avignon, Glanum, Arles, and in Germany with towns, like Staufen, Bad Krosingen, Baden Baden where those Roman legions introduced entire communities to the splendors of aqueducts, amphitheaters and castles. It amazes me how those villages still stand as they were then. Today's traveler has a great opportunity to relive it once again.

Twelve centuries later and Italian family who were not military people but rather traders who traveled across the length and breath of Asia became history along with their most important member, Marco Polo. He came back to Italy with tales of the wonders of the Far East and how they had developed items like explosives and fireworks, beautiful new materials like silk in all sorts of colors.

I too found that traveling throughout the Far East, especially China, was an experience well worthwhile sharing. My trips to China, Japan, Hong Kong and Taiwan were tremendously exciting. No matter how long I stayed, each trip was different and interesting. Like Marco Polo, I am sharing my wonders with you.

Of course when Columbus came to America, he found a land also very different from his native Spain. Although Columbus never did see very much of the Western Hemisphere, he did go back home with unusual and unforgettable memories of the new world. The beginning of this new world which Columbus discovered turned into a world of great promise with tremendous natural resources and potential like he never imagined. In the next five hundred years, the continent changed like no other on earth.

My stories of the trips I took reveal the wonders to be found on this globe. I have tried to give my readers a better insight into what makes this world go round and I hope to continue with my travels and bring you new and exciting stories of my adventures.

Thank you for reading my book.

Eugene Weisberger

My Eight Year Struggle Against Pain

Winter, 2005

I sit in my easy chair on this winter afternoon. The Florida sunshine beams in from the southern window. With the computer on my lap I begin to write of the first time I felt that pain in my back. It was eight long years ago. Much has happened in my life since then. I think of it now, close my eyes as my fingers reach for the computers keys and my mind finds it way back to those eventful times..........

We were about to start on our journey to our seventh and final continent, Antarctica. The year before we had visited Australia, New Zealand and the South Seas. It was an exciting trip, to incredibly beautiful places as were so many others. From my first trips to Europe and then to Asia and Africa, I experienced so many journeys for both business and pleasure. I considered myself fortunate in avoiding accidents and serious illnesses for over a quarter of a century of travel.

Life was good to us until that day in 1996 when a slight swollen gland turned out to be cancer of the parotid gland.

But the pain did not begin then. It was a year later, as we began the trip to the Antarctic that my back pain started. We were in Florida for the winter, as we are this year, all packed up and ready to go. But with each passing day, the pain became more severe. Although I tried to block it out of my mind, there was no hiding its severity. So, for the first time in all my years of travel, I sadly, had to ask Lila to cancel our trip.

During the next four years, there were many surgeries, radiation treatments, and physical therapy sessions, interspersed with periods of recovery and rehabilitation. There were times when my mobility was severely limited as I was restricted to a wheel chair or a walker. Then, of course, I was given many medicines to alleviate my pain. For a period, when I was given steroids they severely altered my personality, and I often became irrational, self-centered and ill tempered. Now in retrospect I realize how my illness effected my family and appreciate how they have stuck by me through all these difficult years. I never knew until lately what a sacrifice they made while I was pulling myself back to physical and mental normality.

But with determination I slowly came back. I knew that I wanted to become a caring member of my family and to enjoy the wonders of life instead of being a difficult person to be with. Then, too. I knew that I wanted to travel once again and thought of the days when that could happen.

Lila knew how important travel was to me. Her story in the beginning of this book tells just a portion of the sacrifice she made for me. One day before one of my operations, she asked me to list all the places I still wanted to visit. It was quite a list. The thought of traveling again gave the motivation to continue despite the pain.

Now eight years later, I thought I would take inventory of places I have been and places that I almost reached. Some places I made despite the pain, others I did not make because of it.

But in each case I tried my best to overcome pain, the struggle, I found the most difficult to content with.

For example, in Iceland one day, I struggled to the top of an extinct volcano with an unusual cave called the cathedral. In the morning I reached this very difficult spot known to hikers for its treacherous terrain. It felt so good to be able to get there. But in the afternoon, I experienced my first failure. I could not make it up to another extinct volcano because it was too steep for me to climb. I had to let my imagine take me to the place my body could not reach. I wrote about that experience in my first book, "The Chinese Walking Stick". The story is called, "Knowing My Limitations." That was the beginning of many "almost made it" experiences.

On the second day of our trip to Belize, Central America, my friend and traveling companion, Marty, and I joined a snorkeling excursion into the Caribbean Sea. I looked forward to snorkeling among some of the most beautiful coral reefs in the world. Next to the Great Barrier Reef in Australia, the Belize Reef is the second largest on the planet. Lila and I had snorkeled along the coast of Australia and around the island of Bora Bora, the year before, and it was spectacular. Now I was eager to see these reefs and the hundreds of schools of fish living there.

I went over the edge of our launch with about a dozen eager snorkelers. I adjusted my face mask to begin what I thought would be a wonderful few hours, and suddenly I found that I could not stay under for any length of time because my lips would not fit over the mouth piece. The water seemed to leak in through the face mask because of my surgery on my neck and face. Marty saw I was having trouble and he immediately came over to me and helped me back to the boat. I sadly had to come out of water, knowing my days of snorkeling were over. For the next three hours I watched while the others had a wonderful time observing those colorful coral reefs. This was another disappointment, not directly caused by my back pain, but a great frustration, nevertheless.

The next year, Joe and I traveled to Egypt while I was still using a wheel chair. Surprisingly it was a very successful trip. I were able to see the temples at Abu Simbel despite the fact the terrain approaching the temple was so rough I could not remain in the wheelchair. After a while I got up out of the chair and walked all the way to the temples of Ramses ll and Queen Nefretari, along the Nile River. It was one of my most memorable traveling experiences.

Then, after returning from our five-day Nile River cruise, we joined a small tour group to visit the giant Pyramids in Giza. We spent several hours going around the sphinx and the three magnificent Pyramids. The final highlight of the trip was hiking down to the bottom of Pharaoh Menkaure's tomb. As we approached the entrance, our tour guide, Leila, said that I would not be able to make it. But, despite the hardships she told me about, I got up out of my wheel chair and made it to the lowest of the royal tombs. I wrote about our trip to Egypt in the Chinese Walking Stick in a story called "Wheeling around the Nile" Sometimes I even surprise myself and do more than I expect to. That day was one of those great ones.

But, then, there were some very difficult times coupled with real disappointments. There was the 2002 European trip to Berlin, Germany and the Czech Republic when my pain got so bad that we was forced to cut our trip short. Joe Burros and I had planned a wonderful travel experience to see some of the eastern European capitols I had never visited. On the itinerary was Berlin, Dresden, Prague and Budapest.

At the Dresden railway station we returned the rented car and took the train to Prague. The seats were very comfortable and I was able to enjoy the ride through the German countryside and along the Elbe River (Moldow River in Czech) River. It was a spectacular ride and by the time I arrived in Prague, I was temporally rejuvenated. But, by the time I walked from our train car to the front of the railway station, my back was aching terribly once again.

I remember that it was necessary for me to sit at the curb of the station while Joe went to call a cab. (my niece, Danya, had given us the name of a cab company to take us to our hotel). So I would say my first view of the wonderful city of Prague was from the curb of its train station; not exactly an auspicious beginning. In a few minutes that felt like an hour, Joe came back with the good news that a cab was on its way. The ride from the station to the hotel was just ten or fifteen minutes. By the time we registered and got up to our room, I just flopped down on the bed, exhausted from pain.

In an hour or two I had recovered enough to go to dinner. We decided to go to a restaurant just a block or two from the hotel. It was a wonderful place and I remember it well. The opera house was on one side of the building and the restaurant was on the other. I thought to myself, wouldn't it be great if we could get to see an opera that night. Under normal conditions, I have so much drive, we would have seen an opera that night despite the long travel day. But this was not a normal day.

After a great dinner with a strolling violinist playing classical music, we immediately headed back to the hotel. The next morning I was determined to see even a little of Prague. So Joe and I took a bus tour throughout that great city. The tour had about four or five sightseeing stops where we could get off and visit various highlights in the heart of this beautiful city. I had read about each of them. I knew the history and what we would be going to see, but I could not find the strength to get off at a single stop. Sadly, I knew the back pain was winning out. But then I found one final burst of energy, and in the afternoon, I did get to see the famous clock in the center of the city.

By the next day, however, I was in such bad shape that we had to make plans to leave. From Prague our itinerary was to visit Budapest, but we never did get to the Hungarian capitol. The story of my retreat from Prague is called Five Days in Hell in my book, The Chinese Walking Stick. We had to fly back from Prague to Paris, and then on to New York, on a emergency basis. There I immediately entered Sloan Kettering Hospital once again, for three more spinal surgeries and five weeks of recovery and antibiotic treatments.

Joe, was just wonderful in making the arrangements with Lila and my pain specialist Nessa Coyle to get me back to New York I called this a strategic retreat in my battle again back pain. And, as General Douglas MacArthur said, upon leaving the Philippine Islands in WW2: I shall return. And so I did! I came back to visit southern France in 2003 and Paris and Germany again in 2004. The stories of those trips are here in this book.

But my wanderlust never ended despite back pain. One day I called Joe and asked him if he would like to go to Yosemite National Park with me. Joe had lived in California for many years and while he was there he often went canoeing and camping in Yosemite. When he would tell me of those trips; of climbing to the top of Half Dome, of hiking along the magnificent valley floor and canoeing the Merced River, I knew I wanted to see, Yosemite, probably the finest of our country's National Parks.

Marty and I had gone to Grand Canyon and had three spectacular days there We never did get to take the donkey ride down to Indian Point. But I always considered that a minor disappointment. We had so many good times on that trip, I look back at it with only happy thoughts and not disappointments. From the canyon we went to Monument Valley, Zion and Bryce National Parks. They were wonderful, exciting days culminating with a stay in Las Vegas. Then a few years later Marty and I went to Yellowstone National Park in Wyoming . That too was spectacular and for the most part, I was able to do the things I wanted to do, with just a little discomfort.

But in 2004 I found the energy and strength to go with Joe to Yosemite. It was a great trip but walking among the giant redwoods took a lot of energy and each day had to be measured in minutes of good time. Fortunately the park had a tram car which took us around the thousand year old sequoias and we saw much of what we had planned.

One of the highlights of visiting Yosemite is to stand on Glacier Point and view the entire panoramic scene, including, El Capitan and Half Dome peaks, as well as the upper and lower Yosemite falls. If I could no longer climb those peaks, at least I would get a marvelous view of them. Joe dropped me off at a spot about two hundred yards from the ledge, and then went off to park our car, while I started to walk toward Glacier Point.

About half way up, there was an overlook and I stopped to 'take in' the incredible views of the falls and the mountains all around me and relax my back which was beginning to hurt by then. After parking the car, Joe met me there and we stood in awe taking pictures and enjoying every minute. In my garrulous way, I often found myself talking to strangers about the only thing we have in common; the love of the wonderful sight we are seeing. I asked a man who just came from the direction of the point, somewhat hesitatingly, "Does it pay to take the hike all the way to the point?" I almost wished he would say, "Oh! No! This is as good as it gets." But that is not what he said, "You have to make it to the end, The view from there is even more spectacular than this."

Slowly but surely I started to hike the remaining distance, determined to see that awesome view. At last I reached the top and spend about one-half hour drinking in what was truly a spectacular sight, indeed. Joe pointed to the many places where he had climbed and camped. He showed he how he reached the top of Half Dome, crawled out to the edge and looked down those six thousand scary feet.

He relived that trip and I shared it with him.

I can always remember how I made it to that point because of a stranger's insistence that "you must get there to see that view." I never knew the man's name nor can I even recall his looks, but this is to thank him for telling me to take that 'one extra step.' That is one accomplishment I am happy to recount.

One last disappointment I struggled with, was during the 2004 trip to Europe. I had planned to go to the top of Mount Belchen in Germany's Black Forest with my friend, Anemone from Munstertal. The day we had planned to reach Mt. Belchen was a clear and bright one. I was sure we were going to get some wonderful pictures from the summit. From the top one gets wonderful views of the entire Black Forest. We took the tram to its station about two hundred or so meters below the top. From the tram terminus we began the hike to the summit of Mount Belchen to take in this most magnificent view of the Black Forest. As we started the walk the air was clear and bright, I was excited that I was going to see this great view. Then about one hundred meter or so, the pain in my back started again and soon became so severe each step became a struggle. It was going to be a battle I would not win but hated to admit it. Anemone saw the look on my face and quietly said, "I think we have gone far enough. Let's go back." And so I never did make it to the top.

Over these eight years, I have struggled to visit places and do things, despite my discomfort and pain. Some goals I have made and others I failed to make.

But, then I would come home and found the strength to write about them.

THE END

978-0-595-35061-2
0-595-35061-5

9 780595 350612